Preface

Each part of this book consists of a general *introduction* to its subject, followed by three chapters, each nominally equivalent to a week's course work. For each chapter the material is structured as follows:

A *text* which introduces the author being studied, provides scientific background information relevant to the author's writing, and comments on the relation of the author's work to the theme of that part. The text can be thought of as brief 'lecture notes', which are intended to stimulate the reader's own thinking about the topic rather than to provide a definitive analysis in themselves.

A *reading list* which specifies the *essential reading* on which the course notes, questions and points for discussion or essays are based. The list includes a group of annotated *related readings* which have been selected on the basis of their direct relevance to the chapter's topic; these may be of use in furnishing additional material for tutorials, seminar discussions or essays, and for providing further insights into the topic during or after completion of the course. The related readings are meant to provide a balanced and more intensive perspective on the topic, but are not designed to be an exhaustive bibliography; the readings cited will themselves supply further bibliographic references.

A set of *questions* which provide a somewhat different coverage of the topic than those in the discussion/essay section, either because they allow for briefer responses or because they focus on scientific and technical aspects of the subject. Although there has been an attempt to furnish sufficient scientific background in the text to enable the reader to answer the questions dealing with technical material in most cases, there will probably be instances where students with insufficient scientific background in particular areas may have difficulty in answering them; the related reading lists should prove helpful here.

A list of *points for discussions or essays*; these are meant to highlight a number of important aspects of the topics and to stimulate the student to a deeper and more wide-ranging analysis than was possible in the brief course notes. With this material there is no clear basis for distinguishing between seminar topics and essay themes; it is hoped that the points suggested will prove suitable for either use (or for tutorial discussion if that format is employed). Needless to say, these points are not an exhaustive listing and are intended to elicit, rather than preclude, additional topics for discussion or essay from the reader.

3

Notes for Teachers

Because the academic recognition of science fiction as a respectable area of investigation is relatively recent, a large body of critical commentary and analysis requiring extensive professional expertize for its interpretation and application does not exist as yet in the field of science fiction studies. Most of the critical works relevant to the subjects of these parts can, therefore, be productively read by students. Consequently, no provision has been made for separate reading lists or teacher texts in this book; teachers will, hopefully, find the bibliographies helpful in organizing the material.

The book was designed primarily for use in tutorials, seminars or discussion groups but, particularly with the introduction of additional material by the teacher, might be appropriate for other formats as well. The two parts are related in topic, but could be used separately if allowance is made for the fact that the course notes for Part 2 involve some continuation of ideas elaborated in Part 1; any problems arising from an isolated use of Part 2, however, could be handled by having students read the course notes of Part 1. The two parts presented here would probably comprise six weeks' work for most participants; since many courses that might make use of the book will last nine weeks, the teacher, by his particular choice of additional material, can exercise a variety of options in designing a course to fit his individual requirements. A few of the possibilities can be touched upon here:

1. A more detailed treatment might be given to the technical content of those areas of scientific theory and research which form the basis for the science fiction speculation — evolution, genetics, embryology, or molecular biology. The fictional readings could be supplemented or preceded by expository scientific texts.

2. A more intensive study might be made of the historical and sociological aspects of the introduction of new scientific ideas. The origins of Darwin's evolutionary theory, its reception, and its influence upon other areas of thought provide a classic example of the interaction of science and society. A contrasting study of the reception of Mendel's work might prove interesting.

3. The topics treated in these course notes might be expanded by further science fiction readings so that each part would last four or five weeks instead of three. Possibilities for extension of Part 1 include additional works by Wells and Stapledon (mentioned in the text and the annotated reading lists), *Hothouse* by Brian Aldiss (London, Sphere) and *Childhood's End* by Arthur C. Clarke (London, Pan; New York, Ballantine). Part 2 could be supplemented with Frank Herbert's *The Eyes of Heisenberg* (New York, Berkley Medallion).

4. Part 1 deals with man as the subject of natural evolution; Part 2 deals with man's conscious intervention in his biological future, a

phenomenon only made possible by the evolution of human intelligence. A third part might consider the problems paradoxically brought on by man's very evolutionary success: over-population resulting from the elimination or reduction of natural biological checks, and ecological threats arising from man's increasing influence on his environment. Essential readings for the science fiction response to the population problem might be Harry Harrison's *Make Room, Make Room* (New York, Berkley Medallion), Anthony Burgess' *The Wanting Seed* (London, Penguin) and John Brunner's *Stand on Zanzibar* (New York, Ballantine). Brunner's book, both for concept and technique, has been one of the more influential science fiction novels of the past decade; one of its secondary themes deals with a program of enforced eugenics, so the novel provides opportunities for interaction with the topic of Part 2 as well. The main problem in using the book is that its length is over 600 pages; depending on the background and interests of participants in the course, *Stand on Zanzibar* could be the basis of a week's work or else be spread over two weeks, with either Harrison's or Burgess' novel completing the three week course, Alternatively, the science fiction treatment of population and ecology could be jointly explored in a single part; the suggestions here would be the Harrison and Burgess novels and John Brunner's vision of ecological apocalypse, *The Sheep Look Up* (New York, Ballantine). Because of length and similarity of technique, *Zanzibar* and *Sheep* would probably not work well together in one part.

Bulwer-Lytton's *The Coming Race* was selected as the opening work because it is one of the earliest instances of a projective use of Darwin's theory. While it is of interest as a prime example of late nineteenth century Utopian didacticism, its most fervent admirer would hardly characterize it as exciting reading; students should be made aware that it does not set the tone for the entire course. In the citation of Olaf Stapledon's *Last and First Men* approximately 50 pages have been eliminated from the assignment; these chapters deal with (Stapledon's imagined) Earth history from 1930 to the present. While these events may have taken place on some Alternate Earth in a parallel time-stream, they did not occur on this one; by omitting these portions of the book, the modern reader will be able to approach the work in the same frame of mind as the members of Stapledon's original audience. The length of *Last and First Men* and its ideational density seemed likely to offer problems for many students if assigned as a single week's work. Since the novel treats in depth the themes of both parts, it appeared feasible to spread the book between the two parts, thus allowing two weeks for reading and discussion. For classes that can handle the book in one week an additional novel might be added from the suggestions given above.

Introduction

This book will examine the manner in which two of the most important developments in modern biology have been reflected in popular fiction. The first part will deal with the literary reaction to Darwin's theory of evolution and, especially, with fictional projections of man's evolutionary future. The second part will deal with the response to science's increasingly detailed understanding of genetics and development, with the awesome potentialities this provides for 'remaking' man. The two parts are interrelated in that Part 1 considers the biological future of man as a continuation of the natural evolutionary processes expounded in Darwin's theory, while Part 2 considers the biological future of man as a result of conscious human intervention in the processes of selection, heredity and development. Of particular concern will be the literary treatment of the human consequences, on the collective and individual level, resulting from these advances in biological knowledge.

Selection of books for the course has been on the basis of their thematic use of biological developments. Such a criterion, of course, is one of the more common (though admittedly oversimplified) methods of characterizing a work as science fiction; and in this sense all the material used as essential reading in these units has been termed 'science fiction', although there are included works which predate the emergence of science fiction as a modern genre (Bulwer-Lytton's *The Coming Race*) and works which have been considered 'mainstream' by a number of literary critics (Aldous Huxley's *Brave New World*).

Science fiction, it may be argued, has performed several related but distinct functions in its treatment of scientific themes. In many cases it has served as a popularizer of scientific theories. These ideas have almost invariably appeared first in scholarly papers and academic books; by their nature such presentations are usually inaccessible for anyone without considerable scientific background. Simplifications, sometimes of a high quality, then follow in popular books, magazines or newspapers, but these frequently require a conscious decision on the part of the reader to be edified. Science fiction, on the other hand, has had a surprisingly heterogeneous audience ranging from the highly educated to the semi-literate; for many of its readers it may well have provided their only exposure to a discussion of certain scientific ideas. In addition, as is true of most forms of popular literature, science fiction is often an unconscious and therefore particularly valuable reflection of the assumptions and attitudes held by the society, in this instance regarding contemporary science. In reading science fiction works more than a couple of decades old, one is frequently struck by this feature of the genre. Moreover, by virtue of its ability to project and dramatize, science fiction has been a particularly effective (and again, for many readers, perhaps the only) means for generating concern and thought about the social, philosophical and moral consequences of scientific progress.

Ironically enough these very features of science fiction which make the genre a newly fashionable area of academic study were those that formerly aroused the scorn of many mainstream critics. When the genre was accorded literary recognition at all, it was frequently dismissed as a mere 'literature of ideas'. *Brave New World*, for example, was often denied (or spared) the science fiction classification because its literary qualities were 'too good for it to be science fiction', an argument whose transparently *a priori* nature did not prevent its wide intellectual circulation. More recently science fiction has gained greater critical acceptance on literary as well as sociological grounds; it has increasingly been appreciated that the form is a twentieth century manifestation of a long tradition of imagination and fantasy, descended from the Gothic, but part of a lineage far older than the generally approved conventions of literary realism. This aspect of the genre is also emphasized in this book — the creative transformation of scientific ideas into artistic symbols and metaphors of the human condition.

The final word on the literary use of science might well be left to one of the authors studied, Aldous Huxley (in his thoughtful contribution to the Leavis—Snow debate over the 'two cultures', *Literature and Science*):

> In the hundred years that have passed since the inventor of science fiction (referring to Jules Verne) embarked on his career, science and technology have made advances of which it was impossible for the author of *From the Earth to the Moon* even to dream. Rooted as they are in the facts of contemporary life, the phantasies of even a second rate writer of modern science fiction are incomparably richer, bolder and stranger than the Utopian or Millenial imaginings of the past.
>
> To the twentieth century man of letters science offers a treasure of newly discovered facts and tentative hypotheses. If he accepts this gift and if, above all, he is sufficiently talented and resourceful to be able to transform the raw materials into works of literary art, the twentieth century man of letters will be able to treat the age-old and perenially relevant theme of human destiny with a depth of understanding, a width of reference, of which, before the rise of science, his predecessors (through no fault of their own, no defect of genius) were incapable.

Part 1

THE FURTHER EVOLUTION OF MAN: THE COMING RACE

Introduction

The publication in 1859 of Charles Darwin's *Origin of Species* — a difficult book of several hundred pages, filled with closely reasoned argument based on a vast array of detailed scientific observations — was an event whose significance was not restricted to professional biologists.

In its impact upon the popular mind; in its radical challenge to established conceptions of man's nature, his purpose, his relationship to God; in its spreading influence upon questions of morality, of economics, and of social and political policy; and in the continuing interest and passion it engendered in its attackers and its defenders, Darwin's theory of evolution was a key intellectual event of the nineteenth century. But an explosion of this order of magnitude, lighting up the conceptual sky for decades, is rarely the work of one isolated theorist. The really spectacular outbursts often draw upon material already lying at hand, the step of creative genius being the realization that the various parts can be hooked together in new and potent combination. The genesis of Darwin's theory exemplifies this nicely.

The idea that development or evolution was a process of fundamental importance in the shaping of the natural world had been gaining credence in the century preceding Darwin. In the field of astronomy evolutionary concepts were being seriously considered by the latter half of the eighteenth century. Immanuel Kant proposed the gradual development of the universe from chaos to organization, the process spreading outward from a central point. Laplace, the great French astronomer and mathematical physicist, proposed in his *Exposition du Systeme du Monde* (1796) his famous nebular hypothesis: The solar system was originally a diffuse cloud of gas which gradually contracted, resulting in an increased rotation. As this process continued, lumps of material flew off like mud from a spinning wheel, forming the planets, while the remaining portion condensed to form the sun. These evolutionary theories in astronomy provoked little controversy.

Around the beginning of the nineteenth century developmental ideas began to be proposed in the study of geology. The prevailing theory was that of Catastrophism, the belief that the earth was relatively recent in origin, something like 6000 years old, and that the structural features which characterize its surface were the result of a series of successive catastrophies of spectacular and rapid action. Both the time scale and the agencies of geological change were axioms of belief that derived much of their strength from the concordance with a literal interpretation of the *Book of Genesis*. The insurgent theory was Uniformitarianism, the idea that all the formations of the earth's crust were accomplished by the same (or similar) causes as those which can be observed in operation at the present moment. Given a vastly expanded time period over which to act, these causes in a quite gradual and unspectacular fashion would themselves account for the earth's geological features without the necessity of special and providential catastrophes.

By the 1830s Charles Lyell's *Principles of Geology* had turned the tide (so to speak) and established the uniformitarian case. The atmosphere in which this controversy was conducted; the apparently ineradicable conflict between scientific and biblical truths; the fear that belief in God, the Bible and the divinely-inspired basis of moral conduct would be undermined if the new scientific theories were accepted; and even the polished rhetoric in which the debate was conducted were, in retrospect, a dress rehearsal for the later, larger and more passionate conflict over evolutionary biology.

The established theory in biology which accounted for the varieties of organic life was that of Special Creation. In earlier centuries it was believed that all existing biological species had been created in their present form at the beginning of earth's history. When geological investigations revealed the presence of fossil forms in the rock layers, with recent fossils (those that bore a close resemblance to modern forms) in the topmost strata and more ancient fossils (those that bore a more distant resemblance to modern forms) in the lower layers, the simple theoretical explanation of a one-time creation had to be abandoned. It was replaced by the concept that there had been a series of special creations of organic life: partial or total destructions of the biota of the earth were accomplished by local or worldwide catastrophes, as in the catastrophist theories of geology; each period of destruction was followed by the creation of a more advanced (or, at least, more recognizably modern) set of living forms.

After the acceptance of the uniformitarian viewpoint in geology much of the support for the catastrophe-dependent special creationist explanations of biological development began to weaken. Moreover, evolutionary ideas of biological change, the gradual transformation of one species into a successor species, had been in the air for a hundred years before Darwin. Buffon in the 1740s and Erasmus Darwin, the grandfather of Charles Darwin, in the 1790s had published speculations which were anticipations of parts of Darwin's theory. The most influential predecessor of Darwin, however, was the French biologist Jean Lamarck; in his *Philosophie Zoologique* (1809) he postulated:

1. the production of an organ with a new function as the result of the need of an animal to adjust itself to changes in the conditions of life (leading ultimately to a new animal);

9

2. the development (or atrophy) of an organ resulting from the extent of its use (or disuse);
3. the transmission to its offspring of those characteristics acquired by the individual.

It is point 3, the inheritance of acquired traits, that has become the characteristic symbol of Lamarckian or neo-Lamarckian theories in biology.

Out of a rather disparate set of stimuli, whose chance elements seem almost to reflect the character of natural selection itself, Darwin's theory slowly took shape. A five year voyage (1831–1836) as an unpaid naturalist aboard *HMS Beagle*, a post chosen after failing to settle upon a satisfactory career in medicine or the church, allowed Darwin to make the wealth of observations that were to prove crucial to his theory. The first volume of Lyell's *Principles of Geology*, which he had been advised by his Cambridge biology professor to buy, read and emphatically disbelieve, he took with him on the long voyage; it converted him to the uniformitarian viewpoint. A few years later his happening to 'read for amusement' Malthus' *Essay on the Principle of Population* turned his thoughts toward the struggle for existence that ensues when a population outgrows its nutritional resources. From these elements and an immense talent for observation, generalization and analysis, Darwin produced the *Origin of Species*.

The tenets of Darwin's theory of natural selection are familiar enough to require only a brief review:
1. Individuals differ slightly from each other; these variations are at least in part hereditary.
2. Those organisms whose variations give them any advantage over their competitors in facing the conditions of life tend to survive longer and produce more offspring, to whom these beneficial hereditary variations are passed on.
3. This 'survival of the fittest' if carried on over a very large number of generations will ultimately produce new species; all species presently existing arose in this fashion from their predecessors.

Where previous evolutionary theories had produced only a few ripples, Darwin's theory of natural selection stirred up a storm of cyclonic dimensions. Twenty-five years of thought, gathering and sifting of data, and laborious marshalling of arguments had gone into the *Origin*. Its detailed reasoning quickly convinced most of the younger generation of biologists, who became enthusiastic supporters of the theory. Although Darwin had studiously avoided bringing a specific discussion of the evolution of man into the *Origin* (Darwin himself only took this step with his *Descent of Man* in 1871) intelligent readers of the book, and its popularizers, readily drew the obvious corollary that man and his fellow primates, the apes, must have descended from a common ancestor. Although the idea that evolutionists were claiming man's descent from the apes was a misconception, the hypothesized common ancestor of both man and ape would undoubtedly look quite ape-like to anyone but a professional anthropologist.

The famous, and somewhat melodramatic, confrontation between Science (represented by the zoologist Thomas Huxley) and Religion (represented, perhaps not quite fairly, by Bishop Wilberforce) that erupted at the meetings of the British Association in 1860 has become the symbol of the forces of controversy that Darwin aroused. (Students might refer to any of a large number of books for details on the Darwinian theory and its reception; particularly readable are *Apes, Angels and Victorians* by William Irvine, and *Darwin and the Darwinian Revolution* by Gertrude Himmelfarb.)

The diversity of attacks from different quarters suggests the wide impact of Darwin's theory. Many theologians, philosophers, moralists and political figures condemned the theory on such grounds as that it robbed the world of its poetry and spirituality; that it interpreted existence, both human and animal, in terms of a soulless mechanism; that man was no more than a beast; and that it vitiated belief in the Bible and therefore in God, his providence and the divine basis of moral codes and behaviour. Cardinal Manning, the leader of the English Catholics, characterized the theory as 'a brutal philosophy — to wit, there is no God, and the ape is our Adam'. Benjamin Disraeli elegantly drew his battle line:

> What is the question now placed before society with glib assurance the most astounding? The question is this — is man an ape or an angel? My Lord, I am on the side of the angels.

By the 1880s the battle had by and large been won, and Darwinian evolution was incorporated into the late Victorian world view. The early reluctance of many fields outside biology to accept the implications of the theory was now replaced by an awesome enthusiasm to apply evolution and natural selection to the problems of areas far removed from biological speciation. The phenomenon of 'Social Darwinism' had arrived. It seemed as though *any* set of beliefs could be supported by recourse to Darwinian principles: Nationalists saw Darwinism as an argument for those governmental measures necessary to a strong state — the 'survival of the fittest among nations'. Advocates of laissez-faire, on the other hand, argued against governmental interference with 'natural selection', particularly in the social and economic spheres.

Militarists found in it the sanction for war, and imperialists the the justification for the conquest of 'inferior races'. Humanistic moralists, though, viewed mankind as a single species sharing a common humanity by virtue of ascent from the purely animal.

Karl Marx saw the theory as showing 'a basis in natural science for the class struggle in history', while John D. Rockefeller declared in a

Sunday-school address:

> The growth of a large business is merely a survival of the fittest . . .
> The American Beauty rose can be produced in the splendor and
> fragrance which bring cheer to its beholder only by sacrificing
> the early buds which grow up around it. This is not an evil
> tendency in business. It is merely the working-out of a law of
> nature and a law of God.

With the exception of biology itself, however, it is perhaps in the
area of literature that evolutionary ideas have had their most long-
standing and still continuing influence. The genre of popular fiction,
in particular, has accommodated evolutionary themes from the days
of the Darwinian controversy to the present time: in the Victorian
popular novel, in the turn-of-the-century scientific romance and in
modern science fiction. The first portion of this course is, in fact, an
investigation of the evolution of evolution in popular literature.

Sources

Gillispie, C. C. (1959). *Genesis and Geology*. New York, Harper

Henkin, L. J. (1963). *Darwinism in the English Novel 1860–1910*.
New York, Russell & Russell

Himmelfarb, G. (1959). *Darwin and the Darwinian Revolution*. Chatto,
London; New York, Norton (1968)

Hofstadter, R. (1955). *Social Darwinism in American Thought*. Boston,
Beacon

Irvine, W. (1955). *Apes, Angels and Victorians*. Cleveland, Meridian

Chapter One
Edward Bulwer–Lytton:
Anticipations of the Coming Race

The Victorian novelist was quick to seize upon the provoking issues of
the day and incorporate them in his work. With its profound impact on
man's view of himself and his relation to God and the world, it might
be expected that Darwinian evolution would become a widely-used
motif in late nineteenth century literature. In fact, the theme appeared
in almost as luxuriant a variety of forms as the original objects of
Darwin's study.

The literary treatment of the Darwinian theme spans two recog-
nizable periods. The earlier one encompasses the years when Darwinism
was a matter of very live controversy, with advocates and critics
passionately debating an issue which had not been resolved in the
public mind. The later period reflects the acceptance and assimilation
of Darwinism into the intellectual world view; evolution could now
be used as the basis for imaginative extrapolation and projection.
Leo J. Henkin in *Darwinism and the English Novel* has produced a
detailed but readable survey of both the earlier and later periods. In
the period of controversy there were first the satires and attacks on
evolution in general, Darwinian natural selection in particular, and
most especially, on the 'Monkey Theory' of man's descent. Then as
the shock waves from Darwinism began to spread there appeared the
novels of religious doubt and spiritual crisis. In many of these an
impressionable young man or woman is seduced into an uncritical
acceptance of atheistic, mechanistic evolutionary theories and only
saved by falling in love with a pious Christian or by hearing the inspired
arguments of an exemplary defender of orthodoxy, most commonly
the local vicar. In many another novel of this period the scenario is
reversed: a sensitive and often devout young man (frequently a clergy-
man) is reluctantly made aware of the truth of Darwinism; his integrity
in refusing to dissemble his new views results in loss of his clerical post,
his social acceptability and his fiancée. A few novels on both sides rose
above this scenario in dealing with the widely-felt spiritual anxiety but
the majority followed the stereotype rather closely. Increasingly
towards the end of the period, a number of authors produced novels
of 'compromise and conciliation' in attempting to reconcile the new
laws of nature with religious belief.

The Coming Race by Sir Edward Bulwer-Lytton was composed
during the controversial period and reflects a somewhat satiric view of
Darwinism (although it also demonstrates an early use of extrapolation
from evolutionary theory, a technique more common in the later

period, which will be discussed in the material of Chapter 2). Brian Aldiss, science fiction author and critic, describes Bulwer-Lytton as having begun life as a 'young Regency sprig who imparted ideas of dandyism to Disraeli', and finishing it 'as one of the dullest pillars of Victorian society'. That Bulwer-Lytton's interest in Darwinism was more than a passing inspiration is shown by several other of his writings. In fact, he revealed true science fictional prescience by satirizing Darwin *before* it became fashionable to do so. In *What Will He Do With It?* published in 1858 (i.e. the year before the appearance of *Origin of Species*) a small-town mayor has presented to the library a two volume edition of 'Researches into the Natural History of Limpets'. This provides the occasion for mild parody — a comic character proposes to lay the foundation for a course in natural history 'and from vertebrated mammiferes . . . gradually arrive at the nervous system of the molluscous division, and produce a sensation, by the production of a limpet'. Darwin had, as it turns out, spent eight years on a study of 'Cirripedia', an order of crustaceans, which was published in 'two thick volumes describing all the known living species, and two thin quartos on the extinct species'. Darwin himself wrote, 'I do not doubt that Sir E. Lytton-Bulwer had me in mind when he introduced in one of his novels a Professor Long who had written two huge volumes on limpets'. In *Kenelm Chillingly* (1873) Bulwer-Lytton has his hero voice many Darwinian ideas, but ultimately has him characterize Darwin as a greater romance writer than Scott or Cervantes. The highly amusing treatment of the 'Wrangling or Philosophical Period of History' in *The Coming Race*, with its great debate over whether the 'An (member of the Coming Race) was descended from the Frog' or 'the Frog was the improved development of the An', is characteristic of the satiric element in his novels.

The Coming Race was published in 1871; Darwin's *Descent of Man* appeared the same year, but could not have influenced the actual writing of the novel. As one of the earliest works to use evolutionary ideas in the depiction of an advanced but human-derived race against which present-day man could contrast himself and, in particular, study himself from a novel perspective, *The Coming Race* was very influential. Indeed, in one guise or another the idea that man might develop into a superior race, or be replaced by one, became a convention of the scientific romance and of later science fiction. Bulwer-Lytton's novel seems to have been one of the earliest to employ such familiar science fictional devices as human-like robots to perform domestic duties and monstrous prehistoric reptiles to arouse the interest of the flagging reader.

The reader of the centenary edition of Bulwer-Lytton's novel is immediately struck by the accuracy (not to say, prescience) of some of his imaginative projections: vril, the agent of terrible destruction, that can also be used to clear paths through mountains and cure disease, prefigures atomic energy; certain intercontinental ballistic tubes of vril can be directed at long range. 'I put it modestly when I say from 500 to 600 miles . . . so as to reduce to ashes within a space of time too short for me to venture to specify it, a capital twice as vast as London'. On the more humane(?) side we have continually piped-in Muzak. And an American (such as the compiler of these course notes) in the aftermath of Vietnam winces on reading of a future in which 'two hundred millions of intelligent citizens, accustomed from infancy to the daily use of revolvers, should apply to a cowering universe the doctrine of the Patriot Monroe'. Finally, a list of the contributions of *The Coming Race* cannot omit mention of the real-world appearance of 'Bovril', the fortified beef beverage.

Sources

Aldiss, B. (1973). *Billion Year Spree.* London, Weidenfeld; Garden City, New York, Doubleday
Henkin, L. J. (1963). *Darwinism in the English Novel.* New York, Russell

Reading

ESSENTIAL

Bulwer-Lytton, E. *The Coming Race,* centenary edition published as *Vril: The Power of the Coming Race.* New York and London, Rudolf Steiner (1972)

RELATED

Aldiss, B. (1973). *Billion Year Spree.* London, Weidenfeld; Garden City, New York, Doubleday
    Probably the best overall study of the science fiction genre, by an important science fiction author. See Chapter 4 for Bulwer-Lytton's and other Victorian visions.
Bellamy, E. (1967). *Looking Backward; 2000–1887.* Harvard, Belknap Press
    The classic American late nineteenth century Utopia.
Butler, S. *Erewhon.* London, Penguin; New York, Signet, NAL
    A Utopian satire of Darwinism, with a number of similarities to *The Coming Race.*
Darwin, C. *The Descent of Man.* (Many editions)
    The detailed application of Darwinian principles to man's origins.
Darwin, C. *On the Origin of Species.* (Many editions)
    The book that started it all off.
Gillispie, C. C. (1959). *Genesis and Geology.* New York, Harper
    A readable and oftentimes amusing account of the British response

to Biblically-unorthodox geological theories; an interesting preview of the reception of Darwinian theory.

Henkin, L. J. (1963). *Darwinism in the English Novel 1860–1910.* New York, Russell & Russell
The definitive work on the appearance of Darwinian themes in English literature. See Chapters I—VIII and XIII.

Himmelfarb, G. (1959). *Darwin and the Darwinian Revolution.* London, Chatto; New York, Norton (1968)
A very well-received treatment of the life and times of Charles Darwin. See especially Chapters XI—XIV and XIX.

Hofstadter, R. (1955). *Social Darwinism in American Thought.* Boston, Beacon
The most thorough treatment of the phenomenon of Social Darwinism; although it focuses on the American scene, the analysis is very useful for the British experience as well.

Irvine, W. (1955). *Apes, Angels and Victorians.* Cleveland, Meridian
A readable account of the lives of Darwin and Thomas Henry Huxley.

Ketterer, D. (1974). *New Worlds for Old.* New York, Anchor/ Doubleday
An unusually sophisticated approach to science fiction criticism; emphasis on the relationship of science fiction to the apocalyptic imagination in general, and to American literature in particular.

Maynard Smith, J. (1958). *The Theory of Evolution.* London, Penguin
A highly readable introduction to modern evolutionary theory by a leading British evolutionary biologist.

Questions

Bulwer-Lytton brings geological references and theories into the novel at many points. How well has he done his scientific homework; are these passages understandable, convincing and consistent? As an armchair geologist is Bulwer-Lytton a Uniformitarian or a Catastrophist? (see the Introduction to this part)

How accurately has Bulwer-Lytton applied the tenets of Darwinian evolution? For example, is he a Darwinian as opposed to a Lamarckian evolutionist? In particular, in terms of the origins of the Vril-ya race and of their mental powers and instinctive control of the vril fluid, are there aspects of Bulwer-Lytton's creation that are inconsistent with Darwinian explanations?

Points for discussion or essays

Discuss *The Coming Race* as a literary example of Social Darwinism. What are the most important political, social and economic ideas that the novel is meant to carry? In terms of effectiveness of presentation and influence on the reader would Bulwer-Lytton have done better to adopt a non-fictional vehicle for his ideas?

The most important single influence in the civilization of the Vril-ya is their discovery and control of the awesome powers of vril. Compare and contrast the transformative influence of vril on the society and politics of the subterranean race with the influence of atomic energy on the corresponding areas of our own superficial (geologically speaking) race.

Bulwer-Lytton portrays the Gy-ei (females) as bigger and stronger than the Vril-ya males, more instinctively in control of the powerful energies of vril, more suited to the scholarly and scientific professions, as well as being the initiators in all amatory relationships. Is Bulwer-Lytton, then, an unrecognized founder of Women's Lib? Discuss Bulwer-Lytton's conscious and unconscious attitudes to women as individuals and as members of society.

David Ketterer in *New Worlds for Old* (p. 97) makes a provocative argument regarding fictional Utopias:

> Words are inherently ambiguous, and the creation of interesting literature depends largely upon the exploitation of this ambiguity. The verbal formulation of a Utopian society involves immediately the introduction of a corrosive equivocation. Considered realistically, the Utopian construct turns against itself to reveal a dystopian underside. To some degree, the satiric attack that the author of a Utopian fiction is implicitly directing against his own society becomes deflected and seeks to undermine the ideal society . . . It would seem, then, that while the Utopian theme negates possibilities of dissonance and narrative complication, the operational techniques and conditions of a literary construct work to reintroduce such conflict and complexity.

Discuss the validity of this argument in the case of *The Coming Race*. Is the society of the Vril-ya a Utopia?

B—1

Chapter Two
H G Wells: The Man of the Year Million

By the last decades of the nineteenth century the Darwinian theory had
become, however reluctantly, an incorporated feature of the Victorian
world view. Novels about the spiritual agonies engendered by the
theory, or further satires of the 'monkey hypothesis', began to be
regarded by the jaded public with the same interest as the Ptolemaic–
Copernican debate. The success of the Darwinian theory resulted in a
veritable adaptive radiation of the novel into new and often exotic
literary environments. Henkin groups these evolutionary excursions
under such titles as 'the anthropological romance' (the prehistoric past,
ape-men, missing links); 'the romance of eccentric evolution' (dealing
with strange aberrations and variant branchings of the evolutionary
tree); and 'the romance of the future' (with its sub-genres embodying
either the idea of progress or that of degeneration). It was in this
burgeoning tradition of the scientific romance that H. G. Wells was to
establish his earliest — and, many critics have said, his most lasting —
literary success.

Herbert George Wells became one of the twentieth century's most
familiar figures; born in 1866, seven years after the publication of
Origin of Species and five years before *The Descent of Man*, he lived
to see the atomic bomb, prefigured in his work, turn into a non-
fictional reality. During his long and immensely prolific life he authored
scientific romances and short stories; realistic novels of lower middle-
class life; fictional and non-fictional portraits of Utopian societies;
polemical treatises on behalf of Fabian socialism, peace and a world
state; a highly successful *Outline of History*; and an encyclopaedic
Science of Life. After an archetypically grisly lower middle-class
childhood and adolescence, Wells received a scholarship to the Royal
College of Science in London. During one of his three years at the
College he studied biology under Thomas Huxley, probably the single
individual most responsible for the ultimate acceptance of Darwinism
in England. Wells' exposure to evolutionary ideas from Darwinism's
most persuasive advocate made the profoundest impression on the
young writer; evolutionary extrapolation was to become a major
thematic element of his early romances.

The future of the human race, both in a biological and a social
sense, remained a preoccupation with Wells for most of his life; he
discoursed upon this question in many non-fictional pieces as well as
in his novels. A particularly important example of Wells' thinking
along evolutionary lines appeared in the *Pall Mall Gazette* in 1893
under the title 'The Man of the Year Million'. In an ironic, startling
and imaginitively thought-out extrapolation, Wells outlined the

possibilities of the future evolutionary development of the human race. It is extremely interesting to compare Wells' treatment of these ideas in the context of a popular magazine article with their development and elaboration in *The Time Machine* and *The War of the Worlds*. One measure of public response to Wells' imaginative projections may be gathered from the satiric poem '1 000 000 AD', which appeared in *Punch* as a response to the *Pall Mall* article.

In *The Early H. G. Wells* Bernard Bergonzi points out that Wells began his literary career as a *fin de siècle* writer. This esthetic and intellectual climate included a sense that 'the nineteenth century — which had contained more events, more history than any other — had gone on too long, and that sensitive souls were growing weary of it'. Victoria's nearly immortal reign and the appearance of peace, security and complacency that accompanied it intensified these feelings in British artistic and literary circles. It seemed at the same time both tedious and vaguely threatening; something large and unknown must be waiting in the wings. The future was looked upon with a mixture of expectation, hope and fear.

In *The Time Machine, The Island of Dr Moreau* and *The War of the Worlds*, the intellectual power and limitless extrapolatory potential of evolutionary ideas were combined with a pervading sense of *fin de siècle* (and *fin du globe*) to produce works whose fascination for the sympathetic reader has not been eroded by the passage of three-quarters of a century. These romances are carefully constructed, informed with an awesome imagination and are complex enough to support a variety of critical interpretations. One (mainstream) critic has said of Wells' early books: 'They are, in their degree, myths; and Mr Wells is a myth-maker'. Another has described *The Time Machine* as a 'poetic social allegory'.

There are a few suggestions that *The Coming Race* influenced Wells. As the Time Traveller lands in the unknown world of 802 701 AD he muses:

What might not have happened to men? . . . What if in the interval the race had . . . developed into something inhuman, unsympathetic and overwhelmingly powerful? I might seem some old-world savage animal, only the more dreadful and disgusting for our common likeness — a foul creature to be incontinently slain.

Highly reminiscent, obviously, of the narrator's situation among the Vril-ya. The Time Traveller soon discovers that the men of the future are physically diminutive, playfully childlike and at the intellectual level of a five year old. 'As I went with them the memory of my confident anticipations of a profoundly grave and intellectual posterity came, with irresistible merriment to my mind.' His unfulfilled anticipations would be those of any reader of *The Coming Race*. One may get some appreciation of the imaginative and narrative powers of the early Wells, however, by comparing *The Time Machine* and *The War of the Worlds* with *The Coming Race* in terms of their purely literary merits. When one recalls that Bulwer-Lytton was one of the most popular novelists of the mid-nineteenth century, Wells' achievement in the deceptively simple form of the scientific romance is all the more apparent.

'It is not what man has been but what he will be, that should interest us', Wells writes in 'The Man of the Year Million', quoting Ruskin. In *The Time Machine*, the lens through which Wells looks at the men of the evolutionary future is bifocal. We see both what man may become when a strenuous natural selection is eliminated (the Eloi) and when a cultural setting, representing the worst aspects of a modern industrial society, becomes sufficiently self-perpetuating and self-reinforcing to serve as the natural selective environment (the Morlocks). In *The War of the Worlds*, Wells' imaginative lens becomes a telescope; the Martians are the 'men' of the future, having evolved on their far older world quite possibly 'from beings not unlike ourselves'. To many of the readers of Wells' day, it must have seemed like the wrong end of the telescope; imperial Britain on the receiving end of interplanetary Social Darwinism, the Green Man's Burden.

With these two novels Wells has taken a momentous step in the literary treatment of the evolutionary theme; for the first time in fiction the evolution of man is portrayed not just as a biological and social phenomenon, but as a cosmic process played against the backdrops of dying planets and a dying sun. And it is this terrifying cosmic perspective, this apocalyptic vision, that has created what are perhaps the two most memorable passages in the science fiction genre — the last twilight of earth in the penultimate chapter of *The Time Machine*, and the opening paragraph of *The War of the Worlds*. In the words of Brian Aldiss: 'Wells is the Prospero of all the brave new worlds of the mind and the Shakespeare of science fiction'.

Sources

Aldiss, B. (1973). *Billion Year Spree*. London, Weidenfeld; Garden City, N.Y., Doubleday

Bergonzi, B. (1961). *The Early H. G. Wells*. Manchester, Manchester UP

Henkin, L. J. (1963). *Darwinism in the English Novel*. New York, Russell

Reading

ESSENTIAL

Wells, H. G. (1893). 'The Man of the Year Million'. *Pall Mall Gazette*, 9 Nov. and the anonymous '1 000 000 AD'. *Punch*, 25 Nov.
Both of these selections are reprinted in *Apeman, Spaceman* edited by L. Stover and H. Harrison (London, Penguin), to whom the author of this book is indebted for the idea of printing them in juxtaposition. They are reprinted as Appendices 1 and 2 to Part 1.
Wells, H. G. *The Time Machine.* London, Pan and Heinemann; New York, Berkley

OPTIONAL

Wells, H. G. *The War of the Worlds.* London, Penguin; New York, Berkley

RELATED

Aldiss, B. (1973). *Billion Year Spree.* London, Penguin; Garden City, N.Y., Doubleday
See Chapter 5 'The Man Who Could Work Miracles: H. G. Wells'.
Bergonzi, B. (1961). *The Early H. G. Wells.* Manchester, Manchester UP
An excellent, appreciative analysis of Wells' scientific romances. See especially Chapters I, II and V.
Henkin, L. J. (1963). *Darwinism in the English Novel.* New York, Russell & Russell
See Chapters IX—XIV, especially XIV.
Mackenzie, N. and Mackenzie, J. (1973). *The Time Traveller.* London, Weidenfeld and *H. G. Wells.* New York, Simon and Schuster (1973)
The newest biography of Wells, voluminous and well-written; of particular interest is the discussion of the influence of Wells' early religious upbringing on the apocalyptic character of his science fiction speculations.
Nicholson, N. (1950). *H. G. Wells.* London, Barker
One of 'The English Novelists' series; a short survey of Wells' writings.
Pritchett, V. S. (1946). 'The Scientific Romances'. In *The Living Novel.* London, Chatto; Westminster, Maryland, Random House (1964)
A brief nine-page appreciation.
Stent, G. (1969). *The Coming of the Golden Age: An End to Progress.* Garden City, N.Y., Natural History Press
The second half of the book is a provocative argument that the very successes of technological man will bring an end to his Faustian strivings.

Wells, H. G. (1934). *Experiment in Autobiography*. London, Gollancz and Riverside, N. J., Macmillan (1934)
In Aldiss' words: 'There have been many books written about Herbert George Wells, but only one really good one, and that he wrote himself'.

Wells, H. G. *The Island of Dr Moreau*. London, Penguin; New York, Berkley
An exploration of the relationship between humanity and animality. The transplant experiments by Dr Moreau can be read as an un-flattering metaphor of the role of a Creator in evolution.

INSPIRATIONAL

Hawley, E. and Rossi, C. (1973). *Bertie: The Life after Death of H. G. Wells.* London, NEL
The spirit of H. G. Wells lives on, and communicates with these two ladies. Students might like to compare and contrast these communications with his earlier work to assay the effect of Wells' spiritual evolution upon his literary abilities.

Questions

What are the most important ways that evolutionary arguments and extrapolations have been used in *The Time Machine* and/or *The War of the Worlds*?

Is there any argument in either of these works that an orthodox Darwinian could reasonably object to?

Points for discussion or essays

Compare the ideas of future evolutionary development appearing in 'The Man of the Year Million' with the handling of these ideas in *The Time Machine* and/or *The War of the Worlds*. Is the novelistic treatment really an improvement over the non-fictional exposition? Why or why not?

Discuss *The War of the Worlds* as an example of, or a reaction against, Social Darwinism.

In *Billion Year Spree*, Brian Aldiss remarks upon the appearance of the 'submerged nation' theme in English fiction. (Disraeli's *Sybil: or The Two Nations* had first expressed this theme, the idea that British society really comprised two distinct nations, the Haves and the Have-nots.) 'This grave moral division lay at the basis of Victorian hypocrisy'. (Aldiss' view, not Disraeli's). In the guilty (?) consciences of many Victorian writers there seemed to lurk a fear that 'the hidden life (awaited) the hour of its revenge', that the exploited and oppressed would have their day in the sun. Discuss the 'submerged nation' theme with respect to the work of Bulwer-Lytton and H. G. Wells.

Present a Marxist critique of *The Coming Race* and *The Time Machine.* Among the points of discussion include consideration of whether Wells' treatment of the evolution of the Eloi and the Morlocks would be compatible with an *orthodox* Marxist viewpoint.

The Time Traveller tells his listeners (and the reader):
> I thought of the physical slightness of the people, their lack of intelligence, and those big, abundant ruins, and it strengthened my belief in a perfect conquest of Nature. For after the battle comes Quiet. Humanity had been strong, energetic and intelligent, and had used all its abundant vitality to alter the conditions under which it lived. And now came the reaction of the altered conditions.

That is, evolution has produced an energetic, intelligent species; this kind of species will transform the environment so as to eliminate the unpleasantly scythe-like selection practiced by nature; in such an environment the qualities that brought man to this point, the qualities that at present he most values, will inevitably deteriorate because there is no selective pressure to maintain them by weeding out the deleterious mutations that must inexorably accumulate in the species. If we are evolutionarily successful, therefore, we are bound to become Eloi. Agree or disagree? Is there anything in Wells' novels that would support a disagreement? (The ambitious student might like to compare this train of reasoning with that of Gunther Stent in *The Coming of the Golden Age: An End to Progress.*)

Compare and contrast Wells' treatment of the evolutionary theme in *The Time Machine* and/or *The War of the Worlds* with that in *The Island of Dr Moreau.*

Discuss the strengths and weaknesses of *The Time Machine* and/or *The War of the Worlds* as literary works (in terms of plot, setting, style, tone, characterization, etc.).

Chapter Three
Olaf Stapledon: The Cosmic Vision

If H. G. Wells is the Shakespeare of science fiction then Olaf Stapledon may be its Milton. In terms of his recognition by the mainstream literary world, however, he is more a 'mute, inglorious Milton'; none of the standard literary references (or the *Dictionary of National Biography*) deal with him. The only biographical mention of him to be found in a major university library, for example, is a brief obituary paragraph in *Who Was Who* (which is the nearly verbatim source of the few details of Stapledon's life prefacing the Penguin editions of his novels).

The comparison with Milton is not, of course, based on an equivalent felicity of literary expression, but rather on the scope and grandeur of Stapledon's epic theme, as exemplified in such a work as *Last and First Men* — nothing less than the meaning of man in his cosmic setting. The traditional novel, if it attempts such a theme at all, most commonly probes the psychological and spiritual nature of a single character whose subjective experiences reflect aspects of the human condition. The examination of the meaning of this individual's existence becomes, therefore, an examination of the meaning of man. The inherent difficulty here is that a single character (or even a small number of characters) can only suggest symbolically rather than represent realistically the almost infinitely complex varieties of human experience. One way of dealing with this dilemma has been to embed the main character(s) in a large-scale setting, filled with a richness of events and of secondary characters, to produce the conviction of a more universal significance. *War and Peace* is probably the best example of a truly epic novel in this sense. Another means of confronting the dilemma has been to abandon altogether the attempt at realistic or naturalistic treatment of individual characters in favor of an explicit allegoric or symbolic representation of man; for example, Christian in Bunyan's *The Pilgrim's Progress* or Adam in Milton's epic *Paradise Lost*. It is Stapledon's achievement to have conceived a totally original form in which to explore the meaning of human existence: a 'novel' in which the 'hero' is not a man, symbolic or realistic, or a small number of men, but Mankind — a Mankind that encompasses seventeen evolutionary transformations from the present fitfully-conscious First Men to the nearly godlike Eighteenth Men; a Mankind that has twice taken root on a new world; a Mankind whose history spans two thousand million years.

In his Preface to *Last and First Men*, Stapledon tells us that the purpose in romancing of the far future is 'to attempt to see the human race in its cosmic setting, and to mould our hearts to entertain new values'. Any attempt to conceive the long drama of man 'must take into account whatever contemporary science has to say about man's own nature and his physical environment'. And further, the aim must not be 'merely to create esthetically admirable fiction, but myth', a myth that is true to its culture in expressing 'richly and often perhaps tragically, the highest admirations possible within that culture'. Stapledon found in science fiction, as H. G. Wells had before him, a framework that could easily incorporate the most recent conceptions of astronomy and of evolutionary biology, that could accommodate unlimited extrapolations of the possibilities and choices that confront mankind, and that could convincingly embody the new forms of myth appropriate to a sceptical and technologically sophisticated twentieth century.

Evolution and transcendence were lifelong preoccupations for Stapledon; first in regard to mankind, and later to sentience or mind in any form. Science fiction evidently continued to prove an agreeable medium for Stapledon's philosophical speculations, for he explored the ramifications of natural and artificial evolution in several additional novels. *Odd John* is one of the most influential treatments of the 'superman' theme in science fiction, an imaginative look at the step beyond *Homo sapiens*. *Sirius* explores the relationship between animality and mind in a dog whose perceptions and intelligence have artificially been raised to the human level. But it is in *Star Maker* that Stapledon's cosmic vision found its most complete expression. Here the growth of consciousness goes beyond even the racial mind of the Last Men to achieve integration with other minded worlds in a galactic mind, and ultimately with other minded galaxies to form the Cosmic Mind that for an eternal instant encompasses all consciousness that has ever existed in time and space — the 'supreme moment of the cosmos' — and in that instant perceives something of the nature of the Creator of the cosmos, the Star Maker. (It would be anti-climactic, if not actually sacrilegious, to reveal the nature of the Star Maker in these brief notes; the reader is directed to the novel itself for the ultimate revelation.) The conceptual sweep of *Star Maker* is almost beyond description; suffice it to say that mankind's agonizing evolution from the budding consciousness of the First Men to the glorious flowering and tragic extinction of the Last Men on Neptune rates about a page in the cosmic perspective of *Star Maker*.

Aldiss considers Stapledon the greatest of Wells' successors and quotes Stapledon's acknowledgement of Wells' influence: 'A man does not record his debt to the air he breathes'. Stapledon frequently used musical metaphors for mankind's history; applying them to Stapledon's work itself, one might say that he has taken the coda of Wells' *Time Machine* — the cosmic viewpoint — and expanded it richly and imaginatively to the dimensions of a symphony (or, perhaps, a Wagnerian opera) in celebration of 'this brief music that is man'.

Of more specific connections to Wells in *Last and First Men*, two are worth special mention. The device of gothic foreshadowing with which Wells so brilliantly preceded the actual description of his Martian invasion (the opening paragraph of *The War of the Worlds*) has been similarly employed by Stapledon. Here, though, there are *two* advance chords — a very brief one near the end of Chapter V (and the first mention of the potential invaders): 'Martians, already watching the earth as a cat a bird beyond its spring . . .' and then the more plangent one at the close of Chapter VIII:

> But elsewhere in the solar system life of a very different kind was seeking, in its own strange manner, ends incomprehensible to man, yet at bottom identical with his own ends. And presently the two were to come together, not in cooperation.

The invasion follows directly.

Readers might also be interested in comparing Stapledon's description of the Great Brains (the Fourth Men, in Chapter XI) — first twelve feet across, later requiring for a cranium 'a roomy turret of ferro-concrete some forty feet in diameter', dependent on an elaborate support system of glass, metal, chemical fluids and attendants, the remainder of the body having become purely vestigial — with Wells' portrayal of the Grand Lunar in *The First Men in the Moon*:

> He seemed a small, self-luminous cloud at first, brooding on his somber throne; his braincase must have measured many yards in diameter . . . At first as I peered into the radiating glow, this quintessential brain looked very much like an opaque, featureless bladder with dim, undulating ghosts of convolutions writhing visibly within. Then beneath its enormity and just above the edge of the throne one saw with a start minute elfin eyes peering out of the glow. No face, but eyes, as if they peered through holes. At first I could see no more than these two staring little eyes, and then below I distinguished the little dwarfed body and its insect-jointed limbs, shrivelled and white. The eyes stared down at me with a strange intensity, and the lower part of the swollen globe was wrinkled. Ineffectual-looking little hand-tentacles steadied this shape on the throne . . . I saw that shadowy attendants were busy spraying that giant brain with a cooling spray, and patting and sustaining it.

These evidences of influence should not be interpreted as unfavorable to Stapledon. The science fiction genre, in fact, encourages the adaptation and further elaboration of ideas introduced by earlier authors; in time these often become conventions of the medium — so, for example, it is no longer necessary to describe the construction of a time machine such as Wells'; the experienced science fiction reader will accept the concept straight away. Wells got to an amazing number of the really important science fictional ideas first; were they out of bounds for his successors, modern science fiction would be rather sparsely populated. Many of the major ideas that Wells missed, Stapledon himself conceived, so that his works have been extremely influential in the development of subsequent science fiction, at least in terms of device and theme, if not of style. A measure of Stapledon's influence is that it has extended to writers whose philosophical and theological positions are the antitheses of his own — nicely illustrated by the reluctant tribute of C. S. Lewis: 'I admire his invention (though not his philosophy) so much that I feel no shame to borrow'.

Sources

Aldiss, B. (1973). *Billion Year Spree.* London, Weidenfeld; Garden City, N.Y., Doubleday

Bergonzi, B. (1961). *The Early H. G. Wells.* Manchester, Manchester UP

Smith, C. (1971). 'Olaf Stapledon: Saint and Revolutionary.' *Extrapolation*, **13**, 1

Reading

ESSENTIAL

Stapledon, O. *Last and First Men.* London, Penguin
See pages 11—23, 46—54, 75—327.

RELATED

Aldiss, B. (1973). *Billion Year Spree.* London, Weidenfeld; Garden City, N.Y., Doubleday
See Chapter 8 'In the Name of the Zeitgeist: Mainly the Thirties'.

Glicksohn, S. (1972). 'A City of Which the Stars are Suburbs'. *The Other Side of Realism.* Edited by T. Clareson. Ohio, Kent State UP
An analysis of Olaf Stapledon's *Last and First Men* and Isaac Asimov's *Foundation* trilogy as reaching toward the limits of the literary imagination.

Lewis, C. S. *Out of the Silent Planet.* London, Pan; Riverside, N. J., Macmillan
The first novel of a theological science fantasy trilogy; a very interesting antithesis to the Stapledonian viewpoint.

Smith, C. (1971). 'Olaf Stapledon: Saint and Revolutionary'. *Extrapolation*, **13**, 1
The case for Stapledon as literary artist.

Stapledon, O. *Odd John.* London, Penguin
The superman theme; a look at man's evolutionary superiors.

Stapledon, O. *Sirius*. London, Penguin

The relationship between animality and mind in a dog whose intelligence has been raised to the human level.

Stapledon, O. *Star Maker*. London, Penguin

The nature and destiny of mind in the cosmos; a still wider perspective on the themes introduced in *Last and First Men*.

Teilhard de Chardin, P. (1959). *The Phenomenon of Man*. London, Collins; New York, Harper

An influential attempt to synthesize evolution and Christianity by a Jesuit geologist, anthropologist and philosopher.

Wollheim, D. (1972). *The Universe Makers*. London, Gollancz; New York, Harper and Row

An internal (and, compared with Aldiss, somewhat parochial) view of science fiction by a long-time science fiction editor.

Questions

To help organize your response to *Last and First Men* it might be useful to construct a genealogical flow chart of the various human species from First to Eighteenth, listing their modes of origin, their most essential characteristics and their most significant achievements.

Select the human species (plural) whose origins are the result of natural (as opposed to artificial) evolution. How consistent are each of these developments with the principles of Darwinian evolution? Which of these species would you consider highly successful, partially successful, or evolutionary dead ends? What are the qualities that distinguish the more successful from the less successful and from the evolutionary failures?

Are Stapledon's Martians more, or less, consistent with Darwinian theory than Wells' Martians? Which group would be more plausible in the light of current knowledge of the surface conditions on Mars?

Among the various future mankinds, are there any that might qualify as Eloi or as Morlocks?

What are the main components of Stapledon's philosophy of man?

Prepare a graph of the 'Evolutionary History of Man'. Along the abscissa place the First through Eighteenth Men. Choose what seems to you a revealing measure of evolutionary development (for example, intellectual capacity, body stature, longevity, sophistication of philosophical discourse, or, perhaps, something more esoteric) and plot this quality on the ordinate on a comparative basis for each of the eighteen mankinds. If suitable the Eloi, Morlocks and Vril-ya might also be included in the graph. It might prove interesting in the seminar to exchange these 'progress' reports and to discuss any significant differences that become apparent.

Points for discussion or essays

Compare and contrast Stapledon's treatment of the evolution of man in *Last and First Men* with that of H. G. Wells in *The Time Machine*. (The comparison should be based on those criteria you think most significant, but should include a discussion of the respective literary strengths and weaknesses.)

Compare and contrast Stapledon's Martians with Wells' Martians. Which war of the worlds has the greater literary impact? Whose Martians are more 'unspeakably nasty'? From which group of Martians do we learn more about ourselves?

Compare Stapledon's treatment of time travel in *Last and First Men* with that of Wells in *The Time Machine*. Which method has the greater potentiality for making important statements about the human condition?

In their novels Stapledon and Wells are expressing, consciously and often unconsciously, their own conceptions of the nature of man and the meaning of human existence. Compare Stapledon's and Wells' philosophies of man.

As both Wells and Stapledon have demonstrated, any intellectually serious attempt at portraying man's long-term evolutionary future must result in profound pessimism. Agree or disagree?

In writing of Kurt Vonnegut in *New Worlds for Old*, David Ketterer observes:

> Science fiction is often attacked because it characteristically lacks human interest and emotional involvement. But this seeming weakness can be regarded as a strength. The point is that, like St John's Apocalypse, the cosmic scope of science fiction and the magnitude of the events or phenomena it treats causes the individual human being to shrink from view. In the science fic-

tional perspective, earthly problems become utterly inconsequential. As it is explained to Malachi Constant in *The Sirens of Titan*, space travel will give him 'an opportunity to see a new and interesting planet, and an opportunity to think about your native planet from a fresh and beautifully detached viewpoint'.

Discuss the validity of this 'detached viewpoint' theory as applied to *Last and First Men*.

Compare Stapledon's treatment of the evolutionary theme in *Last and First Men* with that of his later work, *Star Maker*.

Discuss Stapledon's views of the evolution of sex among his various human species. Are there aspects of the current sexual revolution that correspond to any of Stapledon's conceptions?

In Chapter XVI Stapledon has the spokesman for the Last Men discourse upon their hope of surviving the gradual cooling-down of the sun by annihilating matter to project the earth 'into the neighbourhood of some younger star. Thenceforth, perhaps, he (man) might operate upon a far grander scale. He might explore and colonize all suitable worlds in every corner of the galaxy . . . (p. 313)'. The unexpected disaster about to overtake the sun precludes this, so the Last Men 'are now setting about the forlorn task of disseminating among the stars the seeds of a new humanity' by sending into space sporelike objects with a potential evolutionary bias towards the essentials of human nature (pp. 316–317). C. S. Lewis, a widely respected author and critic, sometimes used science fiction (or science fantasy) as a medium for the exposition of his own Anglican moral philosophy. *Out of the Silent Planet* was published in 1938, and in it Lewis mounts a direct attack on these Stapledonian views (particularly in Lewis, Chapter 20). Some students might like to compare Stapledon's treatment of man's possible emergence into the galaxy with Lewis's.

Approximately three decades separate Wells' treatment of the evolution of man from Bulwer-Lytton's, and the same period again separates Stapledon from Wells. Discuss the extent to which their differing treatments of the evolutionary theme is a reflection of the differing intellectual, social and political climates of their times.

Students who want to range more widely might compare the philosophy of man expressed in *Last and First Men* with that of the Catholic evolutionary philosopher, Teilhard de Chardin, in *The Phenomenon of Man*.

Appendix One

The man of the year million

A Scientific Forecast
H. G. Wells

Accomplished literature is all very well in its way, no doubt, but much more fascinating to the contemplative man are the books that have not been written. These latter are no trouble to hold; there are no pages to turn over. One can read them in bed on sleepless nights without a candle. Turning to another topic, primitive man, in the works of the descriptive anthropologist, is certainly a very entertaining and quaint person, but the man of the future, if we only had the facts, would appeal to us more strongly. Yet where are the books? As Ruskin had said somewhere, apropos of Darwin, it is not what man has been, but what he will be, that should interest us.

The contemplative man in his easy chair, pondering this saying, suddenly beholds in the fire, through the blue haze of his pipe, one of these great unwritten volumes. It is large in size, heavy in lettering, seemingly by one Professor Holzkopf, presumably Professor at Weissnichtwo. 'The Necessary Characters of the Man of the Remote Future Deduced from the Existing Stream of Tendency' is the title. The worthy Professor is severely scientific in his method, and deliberate and cautious in his deductions, the contemplative man discovers as he pursues his theme, and yet the conclusions are, to say the least, re-markable. We must figure the excellent Professor expounding the matter at great length, voluminously technical, but the contemplative man — since he has access to the only copy — is clearly at liberty to make such extracts and abstracts as he chooses for the unscientific reader. Here, for instance, is something of practicable lucidity that he con-siders admits of quotation.

'The theory of evolution', writes the Professor, 'is now universally accepted by zoologists and botanists, and it is applied unreservedly to man. Some question, indeed, whether it fits his soul, but all agree it accounts for his body. Man, we are assured, is descended from ape-like ancestors, moulded by circumstances into men, and these apes again were derived from ancestral forms of a lower order and so up from the primordial protoplasmic jelly. Clearly then, man, unless the order of the universe has come to an end, will undergo further modification in the future, and at last cease to be man, giving rise to some other type of animated being. At once the fascinating question arises. What will this being be? Let us consider for a little the plastic influences at work upon our species.

'Just as the bird is the creature of the wing, and is all moulded and modified to flying, and just as the fish is the creature that swims, and has had to meet the inflexible conditions of a problem in hydro-dynamics, so man is the creature of the brain; he will live by intelligence, and not by physical strength, if he lives at all. So that much that is purely 'animal' about him is being, and must be, beyond all question, suppressed in his ultimate development. Evolution is no mechanical tendency making for perfection according to the ideas current in the year of grace 1892; it is simply the continual adaptation of plastic life for good or evil, to the circumstances that surround it . . . We notice this decay of the animal part around us now, in the loss of the teeth and hair, in the dwindling hands and feet of men, in their smaller jaws, and slighter mouths and ears. Man now does by wit and machinery and verbal agreement what he once did by toil; for once he had to catch his dinner, capture his wife, run away from his enemies, and continually exercise himself, for love of himself, to perform these duties well. But now all this is changed: Cabs, trains, trams, render speed unnecessary; the pursuit of food becomes easier; his wife is no longer hunted, but rather in view of the crowded matrimonial market, seeks him out. One needs wits now to live, and physical activity is a drug, a snare even: it seeks artificial outlets and overflows in games. Athleticism takes up time and cripples a man in his competitive exami-nations and in business. So is your fleshy man handicapped against his subtler brother. He is unsuccessful in life, does not marry. The better adapted survive.'

The coming man, then, will clearly have a larger brain, and a slighter body than the present. But the Professor makes one exception to this. 'The human hand, since it is the teacher and interpreter of the brain, will become constantly more powerful and subtle as the rest of the musculature dwindles.'

When in the physiology of these children of men, with their ex-panding brains, their great sensitive hands, and diminishing bodies, great changes were necessarily worked. 'We see now', says the Pro-fessor, 'in the more intellectual sections of humanity an increasing sensitiveness to stimulants, a growing inability to grapple with such a matter as alcohol, for instance. No longer can men drink a bottle full of port: some cannot drink tea; it is too exciting for their highly-wrought nervous systems. The process will go on, and the Sir Wilfrid Lawson of some near generation may find it his duty and pleasure to make the silvery spray of his wisdom tintinnabulate against the tea-tray. These facts lead naturally to the comprehension of others. Fresh raw meat was once a dish for a king. Now refined persons scarcely touch meat unless it is cunningly disguised. Again, consider the case of turnips; the raw root is now a thing almost uneatable, but once upon a time a turnip must have been a rare and fortunate find, to be torn up with delirious eagerness and devoured in ecstasy. The time will come when the change will affect all the other fruits of the earth.

Even now only the young of mankind eat apples raw — the young always preserving ancestral characteristics after their disappearance in the adult. Someday, boys even will regard apples without emotion. The boy of the future one must believe, will gaze on an apple with the same unspeculative languor with which he now regards a flint in the absence of a cat.

'Furthermore, fresh chemical discoveries came into action as modifying influences upon men. In the prehistoric period even, man's mouth had ceased to be an instrument for grasping food; it is still growing continually less prehensile, his front teeth are smaller, his lips thinner and less muscular; he has a new organ, a mandible not of irreparable tissue, but of bone and steel — a knife and fork. There is no reason why things should stop at the partial artificial division thus afforded; there is every reason, on the contrary, to believe my statement that some cunning exterior mechanism will presently masticate and insalivate his dinner, relieve his diminishing salivary glands and teeth, and at last abolish them altogether.'

Then what is not needed disappears. What use is there for external ears, nose, and brow ridges now? The two latter once protected the eye from injury in conflict and in falls, but in these days we keep on our legs, and at peace. Directing his thoughts in this way, the reader may presently conjure up a dim, strange vision of the latter-day face: 'Eyes large, lustrous, beautiful, soulful; above them no longer separated by rugged brow ridges, is the top of the head, a glistening, hairless dome, terete and beautiful; no craggy nose rises to disturb by its unmeaning shadows the symmetry of that calm face, no vestigial ears project; the mouth is a small, perfectly round aperture, toothless and gumless, jawless, unanimal, no futile emotions disturbing its roundness as it lies, like the harvest moon or the evening star, in the wide firmament of face.' Such is the face the Professor beholds in the future.

Of course parallel modifications will also affect the body and limbs. 'Every day so many hours and so much energy are required for digestion; a gross torpidity, a carnal lethargy, seizes on mortal men after dinner. This may be and can be avoided. Man's knowledge of organic chemistry widens daily. Already he can supplement the gastric glands by artificial devices. Every doctor who administers physic implies that the bodily functions may be artificially superseded. We have pepsine, pancreatine, artificial gastric acid — I know not what like mixtures. Why, then, should not the stomach be ultimately superannuated altogether? A man who could not only leave his dinner to be cooked, but also leave it to be masticated and digested, would have vast social advantages over his food-digesting fellow. This is, let me remind you here, the calmest, most passionless, and scientific working out of the future forms of things from the data of the present. At this stage the following facts may perhaps stimulate your imagination. There can be no doubt that many of the arthropods, a division of animals more ancient

33

and even now more prevalent than the vertebrata, have undergone more phylogenetic modification' — a beautiful phrase — 'than even the most modified of vertebrate animals. Simple forms like the lobsters display a primitive structure parallel with that of the fishes. However, in such a form as the degraded *Chondracanthus* the structure has diverged far more widely from its original type than in man. Among some of these most highly modified crustaceans, the whole of the alimentary canal, that is, all the food-digesting and food-absorbing parts form a useless solid cord: The animal is nourished — it is a parasite — by absorption of the nutritive fluid in which it swims. Is there any absolute impossibility in supposing man to be destined for a similar change; to imagine him no longer dining with unwieldly paraphernalia of servants and plates, upon food queerly dyed and distorted, but nourishing himself in elegant simplicity by immersion in a tub of nutritive fluid?

'There grows upon the impatient imagination a building, a dome of crystal, across the translucent surface of which flushes of the most glorious and pure prismatic colours pass and fade and change. In the centre of this transparent chameleon-tinted dome is a circular marble basin filled with some clear, mobile, amber liquid, and in this plunge and float strange beings. Are they birds?

'They are descendants of man — at dinner. Watch them as they hop on their hands — a method of progression advocated already by Bjornsen — about the pure white marble floor. Great hands they have, enormous brains, soft, liquid, soulful eyes. Their whole muscular system, their legs, their abdomens, are shrivelled to nothing, a dangling degraded pendant to their minds.'

The further visions of the Professor are less alluring.

'The animals and plants die away before men, except such as he preserved for his food or delight, or such as maintain a precarious footing about him as commensals and parasites. These vermin and pests must succumb sooner or later to his untiring inventiveness and incessantly growing discipline. When he learns (the chemists are doubt-less getting toward the secret now) to do the work of chlorophyll without the plant, then his necessity for other animals and plants upon the earth will disappear. Sooner or later, where there is no power of resistance and no necessity, there comes extinction. In the last days man will be alone on the earth, and his food will be won by the chemist from the dead rocks and the sunlight.

'And — one may learn from the full reason in that explicit and painfully right book, the *Data of Ethics* — the irrational fellowship of man will give place to an intellectual cooperation, and emotion fall within the scheme of reason. Undoubtedly it is a long time yet, but a long time is nothing in the face of eternity, and every man who thinks of these things must look eternity in the face.'

Then the earth is ever radiating away heat into space, the Professor reminds us. And so at last comes a vision of earthly cherubim, hopping heads, great unemotional intelligences, and little hearts, fighting together perforce and fiercely against the cold that grips them tighter and tighter. For the world is cooling — slowly and inevitably it grows colder as the years roll by. 'We must imagine these creatures', says the Professor, 'in galleries and laboratories deep down in the bowels of the earth. The whole world will be snow-covered and piled with ice; all animals, all vegetation vanished, except this last branch of the tree of life. The last men have gone even deeper, following the diminishing heat of the planet, and vast steel shafts and ventilators make way for the air they need.'

So with a glimpse of these human tadpoles, in their deep close gallery, with their boring machinery ringing away, and artificial lights glaring and casting black shadows, the Professor's horoscope concludes. Humanity in dismal retreat before the cold, changed beyond recognition. Yet the Professor is reasonable enough, his facts are current science, his methods orderly. The contemplative man shivers at the prospect, starts up to poke the fire, and the whole of this remarkable book that is not written vanishes straight away in the smoke of his pipe. This is the great advantage of this unwritten literature: There is no bother in changing the books. Our contemplative man consoles himself for the destiny of the species with the lost portion of Kublai Khan.

Appendix Two

1 000 000 AD
Anonymous

What, a million years hence will become of the *Genus
    Humanum,* is truly a question vexed;
At that epoch, however, *one* prophet has seen us
    Resemble the sketch annexed.

For a Man undergoes Evolution ruthless,
    His skull will grow 'domelike, bald, terete',
And his mouth will be jawless, gumless, toothless —
    No more will he drink or eat!

He will soak in a crystalline bath of pepsine,
    (No ROBERT will then have survived, to wait,)
And he'll hop on his hands as his food he steps in —
    A quasi-cherubic gait!

No longer the land or the sea he'll furrow;
    The world will be withered, ice-cold, dead.
As the chill of Eternity grows, he'll burrow
    Far down underground instead.

If the *Pall Mall Gazette* has thus been giving
    A forecast correct of this change immense,
Our stars we may thank, then, that *we* shan't be living
    A million years from hence!

Part 2
GENETIC ENGINEERING: BRAVE NEW WORLDS

Introduction

By the latter part of the nineteenth century Darwinian evolution had been assimilated into the general world view and had become a fundamental framework for biological thought and research. Its scientific pre-eminence, however, did not mean that the theory was completely satisfactory as it stood. Granting the sometimes direct, sometimes subtle competition within and among species, and the consequent winnowing by natural selection of the fitter individuals in that struggle for existence, a large difficulty remained. In the early formulations of the theory it was envisaged that natural selection acted to preserve favorable variations; i.e. all individuals of a species vary, those with the more favorable variations survive longer and produce more offspring to whom these advantageous characteristics are passed on. But *how* do variations, beneficial or deleterious, come about in the first place? This type of question is hardly trivial; depending on the answer provided, the development of man may be interpreted as resulting from blind chance, or from a mechanical response to the environment, or from some purposive, directive force in nature.

Whatever the origin of variations, a further unsolved problem was the manner of their hereditary transmission. Consider, for example, a 'Darwinian' giraffe at a time when the species might have had only moderately long necks. The environment would seem to favor those rare individuals with a somewhat longer neck (who would get a larger share of the succulent arboreal vegetation than their shorter-necked fellows, etc.). But this rare long-necked giraffe will (statistically speaking) mate with a shorter-necked companion; surely their offspring will have neck lengths somewhere between those of their parents. A few more matings and this favorable variation will be swamped out altogether rather than preserved. In a vain attempt to answer this objection Darwin himself was reduced to an almost Lamarckian view of the inheritance of acquired characteristics, differing only to the extent that Darwin employed his intellectual resources in hypothesizing an elaborate (and quite erroneous) mechanism for such a mode of inheritance. Ironically enough, at the very time that Darwin was agonizing over these difficulties the work that could have resolved them was lying unread in the pages of the *Proceedings of the Natural Science Society of Brünn* (1866), an unfortunately obscure provincial journal. The work was that of Gregor Mendel, and went unrecognized until

1900 when three separate scientists unknowingly duplicated Mendel's researches, only afterwards discovering Mendel's priority. This work became the foundation of the modern science of genetics.

The new theory postulated the existence of 'particulate' hereditary determinants, the genes. In the simplest cases it was assumed that two of these factors, one from each of the parents, controlled the appearance of a trait; for example, the color of a flower or the shape of a leaf. If both parents contributed to the offspring, via their respective germ (reproductive) cells, exactly the same form of the gene controlling a particular trait, then the organism would invariably demonstrate in that trait the phenotype (appearance) characteristic of that particular form of the gene. If the two parents each contributed to the offspring a different form of the gene, most frequently the organism would display the phenotype characteristic of only one of the two forms of the gene; this form of the gene was termed a 'dominant gene' for obvious reasons. The other form of the gene, whose influence was seemingly submerged, was termed a 'recessive gene'. Of great importance, however, was the fact that if the offspring received from each of the parents the same recessive form of the gene, the organism would evidence the phenotype characteristic of that (usually hidden) form of the gene.

With this reasoning the question of why favorable variations are not swamped out by blending is apparent. If the favorable variation is due to a dominant gene, on the average half the offspring of that organism will receive the dominant gene and will automatically show the favorable trait which can then be passed on in the same manner to future generations. If the favorable variation is due to a recessive gene, then in an organism possessing this advantageous characteristic both of the genes that control the trait must be of the recessive type. In general the offspring, getting only one such recessive gene from a parent, will not show the favorable trait but will be able to transmit this recessive gene, unexpressed but intact, to some of its progeny. If some member of a future generation receives two of these recessive genes it will once again display the favorable phenotype characteristic of this gene. In other words, the genes apparently preserve their individual identities (as if they were particulate in nature) throughout any number of generations.

The rare exception to this rule of the continued integrity of the genes turns out to provide the basis for the origin of new variations. If, on very infrequent occasions, a new form of a gene appears (a 'mutation'), from that point on it behaves exactly as any other dominant or recessive gene. Its transmission to future generations proceeds in the usual fashion and its expression in the appearance of the associated trait is judged by the agency of natural selection. The young science of genetics thus supplied a remarkably satisfying explanation for the driving force of evolution: hereditary factors whose *almost* invariable nature preserved favorable variations intact across innumerable successive generations, but whose extremely rare changes of identity provided the opportunity for the appearance of new variations.

From these beginnings the field of genetics developed rapidly; by the early 1930s the simple crosses of Mendelism had been replaced by the sophisticated conceptual apparatus of equilibrium and population genetics. A formidable array of mathematical techniques could be applied to the analysis of the frequencies and interactions of genes in breeding populations, taking into account such factors as differing mutation rates, natural and artificial selections, migration and mixing of populations, and even chance elements. What may not be apparent about mathematical genetics, however, is that most of its spectacular achievements have been based on a purely formal and abstract conception of the gene as the 'hereditary unit'. Knowledge of the real physical composition of the gene — the actual nature of the hereditary material — was not essential to mathematical analysis or successful prediction of patterns of inheritance and of evolutionary change in populations.

To anyone who considered, even faintly, the possibility of improving upon the seemingly blind and wasteful process of chance variation plus natural selection, or who hoped to alleviate any of the miseries caused by less-than-favorable genetic variations in living human beings, an understanding of the hereditary material was paramount. The first influential hypothesis as to the biological location of the basis of inheritance came as early as 1866, the year in which Mendel published his unnoticed researches; it was postulated that the nucleus of the cell was responsible for the transmission of the hereditary features of an organism. By the mid 1880s it was a tenable, if untested, hypothesis that the basis of inheritance was to be found in the chromosomes, threadlike bodies that are clearly visible in the nucleus during certain phases of the life cycle of the cell. In 1903 this belief received very persuasive support when it was realized that the behavior of Mendel's newly rediscovered (and, of course, invisible) genes was strikingly parallel to the behavior of the easily observable chromosomes in the nucleus. A consistent picture soon emerged: The chromosomes in the cells of living organisms occur in pairs; humans, for example, have 46 chromosomes or 23 pairs. But the human sperm and egg cells contain only 23 chromosomes, one member from each pair, so that on uniting to form a fertilized egg the characteristic number of chromosomes is restored. These chromosomes carry the genes; of the two genes that control the appearance of simple traits, one is present in each member of the chromosome pair. All the cells of an organism are descendants of the original fertilized egg and so presumably carry the identical genes.

During the following two decades many of the details of this outline began to be filled in. Work on the apparently unlikely organism, *Drosophila* (the fruit fly), revealed that certain genes seem to be linked together in their inheritance. And, neatly enough, it soon became clear that the number of these theoretically derived 'linkage groups' was the same as the number of chromosome pairs in the cell. Using rather complex techniques, geneticists could reliably 'map' the genes of a linkage group; that is, determine which genes were located near each other and which genes further away. The linear order of these genes with respect to each other on the linkage map was believed to reflect their actual arrangement in the chromosome. Because of the elaborate breeding procedures required for this kind of information, genetic maps of *Drosophila* are far easier to obtain than for man, but the principles involved are identical.

Thus the previously separate fields of genetics and cell biology had come together to produce a highly convincing picture of the nature of the hereditary process. The basis of Darwinian variations, upon which natural selection operated, was now understood. In scientific terms, at least, a number of widely-held philosophical notions about evolution were rendered highly implausible. Any acquired characteristics of an organism, no matter how desirable, seemed unlikely to be able to exert a *specific* effect on the chromosomes or genes of the germ cells. Similarly, the rather comforting idea that there was some creative or directive force in nature behind evolution received no support from an increased understanding of genetics; to the contrary, the occurrence of mutations, the basis of new evolutionary developments, was statistically random, and only rarely beneficial. So by 1930 it was evident that heredity and evolution had a reasonably well understood material basis; and that if man did not want to leave his potential improvement to a mechanical natural selection acting upon the results of chance mutational events, most of which were deleterious, he must consider acting upon that hereditary material and/or the developmental process that derives from it as an enlightened, conscious agent of evolution. Within the space of two years this awesome possibility and the equally awesome dangers had attracted the diverse imaginations of Olaf Stapledon and Aldous Huxley.

Sources

Darlington, C. D. (1960). *Darwin's Place in History.* Oxford, Blackwell; Riverside, N. J., Macmillan (1961)

Dunn, L. C. (1965). *A Short History of Genetics.* New York, McGraw-Hill

Moore, J. A. (1972). *Heredity and Development.* London, Oxford UP

Chapter Four
Olaf Stapledon: Man Maker

At the beginning of the seventeenth century, Francis Bacon laid the ideological groundwork for an activist science in which the control of nature would lead to the relief of man's estate. By the twentieth century the successes of that science lent support to a rather more radical suggestion: that the improvement of man's estate might best be accomplished by the biological improvement of man himself. The theoretical basis for such a possibility had been provided, at least in outline, by the new insights of evolutionary theory, genetics and cell biology. The question now was whether, and in what way, this knowledge should be put to use.

There was, of course, the widely-held opinion that since natural evolution had brought about man's present eminence, the further improvement of man should be left to the same agency. But those who pressed for man to intervene in the shaping of his own nature raised two objections. The first was that nature was blind, wasteful and — perhaps worst of all now that man had evolved enough to be impatient — slow. Variations or mutations, the raw material of evolution, occur randomly, not by any specific response of the organism to its own needs or to the pressures of the environment. And the vast majority of mutations are harmful rather than progressive. The human organism in its present state is extraordinarily complex and highly integrated; expecting a chance mutation to be advantageous is somewhat like reaching into a television set, reconnecting a couple of leads at random, and hoping for an improvement in the picture. Corroboration of this may be seen in any medical textbook on inherited disorders, which will list hundreds of genetic abnormalities such as hemophilia, color blindness, alkaptonuria, phenylketonuria, etc. Moreover, any major improvement in a species is generally the result of a large number of mutations accumulated over immensely long periods of time; for example, modern man does not differ in any biologically significant way from his Cro-Magnon ancestors of 35 000 years ago. There seemed no reason to believe that nature would improve either her aim or her speed in response to Man's newly heightened expectations.

The second objection to a *laissez-faire* evolution was that in reality man *was* interfering with the natural process, not by a policy of conscious improvement but rather by one of unwitting degeneration. Man's evolutionary success, it was argued, had given him the power of artificially blunting the selective aspects of nature. For the most human of reasons, man had improved both medical care and social services; individuals with unfavorable genetic variations who previously would not have survived to reproductive age, or who would have been only marginally reproductive, were now being enabled to procreate more extensively. On the individual level this might be tolerable, but on the long-term evolutionary level this would inevitably increase the frequency of deleterious genes in the human population.

The earliest and most influential exponent of a program to face these difficulties was Francis Galton (a cousin of Charles Darwin interestingly enough), who advocated a policy of deliberate genetic improvement of the human race and introduced the word *eugenics*. There are two distinguishable eugenic strategies: the 'positive' approach which might be directed to the planned improvement of the human species by breeding for superior individuals, and the 'negative' approach which would discourage the proliferation of the more extreme inherited defects (It should be mentioned here that more recent genetic knowledge has called into question a number of assumptions on which these simple eugenic arguments were based, particularly in the case of the negative strategy, making the possibility of eugenic improvement by selective breeding far more problematic than it might first appear. Theodosius Dobzhansky's *Mankind Evolving* and John Maynard Smith's 'Eugenics and Utopia' do an especially good job of discussing this point.)

It might be expected that writers who based many of their literary projections on the scientific concerns of their time would find in eugenic themes a topic for exploration. While not focusing any of his early romances upon this question, H. G. Wells did advocate the policy of preventative eugenics in his prescription for *A Modern Utopia*. In *Last and First Men*, Olaf Stapledon gave considerable thought to eugenic practices. One of the causes of the decline of the First Men, for example, was their lack of an effective eugenic program:

> In primitive times the intelligence and sanity of the race had been preserved by the inability of its unwholesome members to survive. When humanitarianism came into vogue, and the unsound were tended at public expense, this natural selection ceased. And since these unfortunates were incapable alike of prudence and of social responsibility, they procreated without restraint, and threatened to infect the whole species with their rottenness. During the zenith of Western Civilization, therefore, the sub-normal were sterilized. But the latter-day worshippers of Gordelpus regarded both sterilization and contraception as a wicked interference with the divine potency. Consequently the only restriction on population was the suspension of the newborn from aeroplanes, a process which, though it eliminated weaklings, favoured among healthy infants rather the primitive than the highly developed. Thus the intelligence of the race steadily declined. And no one regretted it. (Chapter IV, 4)

Much later, a race of the Third Men developed a more positive interest:

> Mating, at least among the more devout sort of women, began to be influenced by the desire to have children who should be of outstanding musical brilliance and sensitivity. Biological sciences were rudimentary, but the general principle of selective breeding was known. Within a century this policy of breeding for music, or breeding 'soul', developed from a private idiosyncrasy into a racial obsession. (Chapter X, 2)

The end result of this particular practice, however, was somewhat discouraging:

> 'Under the stimulus of music which was not to their taste they were apt to run amok and murder the performers.'

After the light relief of providing for the evolutionary appearance of what one might term 'aeroplane hangars' in the first example and activist music critics in the second, Stapledon presents an extremely thought-provoking exploration of the limits, both biological and philosophical, to which selective breeding might be pushed. In this instance the breeding is being applied to animals, but its importance lies in the light it reflects on the role of man as an emerging controller of evolution.

As with so many of Stapledon's ideas, this is but the prelude to a far larger conception. To alter the evolutionary nature of a species in any really significant way

> much more was needed than the rule-of-thumb principles of earlier breeders. It took this brightest of all the races of the third species many thousands of years of research to discover the more delicate principles of heredity, and to devise a technique by which the actual hereditary factors in the germ could be manipulated. (Chapter X, 3)

In seizing upon this conception, Stapledon was extrapolating from the most recent scientific work (or anticipating it). In 1927 it was shown that the frequency of occurrence of mutations could be tremendously increased by the exposure of reproductive cells to large doses of x-rays. Further research showed that similar effects could be obtained from a number of other agents as well, e.g. cathode rays, gamma rays, ultraviolet light and, later, certain chemicals. The mutations produced in this manner are of exactly the same kind as those produced naturally. What these artificial mutagens do is to greatly increase the *rate* at which random mutations occur, not to make the mutations any more specific or selective. Even with this extremely important qualification, however, the import of the work was clear: the effect of these mutagens must be due to their interaction with the physical—chemical structure of the gene. If scientists could uncover the actual structure of the gene and understand its functioning in detailed chemical terms, it might indeed be possible in the future to engage in specific, controlled manipulation of the hereditary material.

In Stapledon's day this was, at best, still a faint promise; detailed knowledge of the chemical and physical structure of the gene seemed a distant prospect. Yet this was sufficient foundation for Stapledon's imaginative edifice. With his mountain-top perspective the Neptunian narrator of *Last and First Men* need not describe the actual details of the manipulative process; he establishes its general plausibility, and the reader follows him from there. And with complete confidence Stapledon leads that reader into the earliest — and what may still be the bravest — new world of genetic engineering.

Sources

Darlington, C. D. (1964). *Genetics and Man.* London and Riverside, N. J., Macmillan

Dobzhansky, T. (1962). *Mankind Evolving.* New Haven, Yale UP

Sturtevant, A. H. (1966). *A History of Genetics.* London and New York, Harper

Reading

ESSENTIAL

Stapledon, O. *Last and First Men.* London, Penguin

RELATED

Blacker, C. P. (1952). *Eugenics: Galton and After.* London, Duckworth
A look at Galton's life and work followed by an account of the eugenics movement up to the early 1950s by the General Secretary of the Eugenics Society.

Darlington, C. D. (1964). *Genetics and Man.* London and Riverside, N.J., Macmillan
A highly readable, non-technical treatment by a leading British biologist.

Dobzhansky, T. (1962). *Mankind Evolving.* New Haven, Yale UP
A highly readable, non-technical treatment by a leading American biologist.

Dunn, L. C. (1965). *A Short History of Genetics.* New York, McGraw-Hill
A chronological and slightly more technical treatment of the field.

Ginsberg, M. (1956). 'The Claims of Eugenics'. In *On the Diversity of Morals*. London, Heinemann

A sociologist's analysis of a number of eugenic arguments; the author finds that the 'crude methods' of the eugenists do not enable us to estimate the relative significance of environmental and genetic factors in social life.

Maynard Smith, J. (1972). 'Eugenics and Utopia'. In *On Evolution*. Edinburgh, Edinburgh UP

A fine short treatment of the difficulties involved in attempts at constructing genetic Utopias; concludes that at the moment eugenic arguments only distract attention from more urgent social questions.

Moore, J. A. (1972). *Heredity and Development*. London, Oxford UP

A widely-used textbook on genetics and embryology directed at first-year university students in biology.

Shelley, M. *Frankenstein*. Oxford, Everyman and Oxford; New York, Bantam

An earlier example of the influence of contemporary developments in biology (here, Galvanic electricity) on literature. Aldiss considers *Frankenstein* as the origin of modern science fiction.

Simpson, G. (1953). *The Major Features of Evolution*. New York, Columbia UP

A detailed study of generalizable trends in evolution by an eminent American evolutionary biologist.

Sturtevant, A. H. (1966). *A History of Genetics*. London and New York, Harper

A detailed, technical history of the field.

Questions

How consistent are the following Stapledonian situations with modern genetic theory?

1. 'But the revival (i.e. of the Patagonian race by the propagation of the seed of the Divine Boy, a unique biological "sport", or throwback to an earlier vitality) was not permanent. The descendants of the prophet prided themselves too much on violent living. Physically, sexually, mentally, they over-reached themselves and became enfeebled. Moreover, little by little the potent strain was diluted and overwhelmed by intercourse with the greater volume of the innately 'senile', so that, after a few centuries, the race returned to its middle-aged mood.'

2. (Referring to the decline of the Second Men after their self-destructive victory over the Martians) 'For, in a species in which the lower functions were so strictly disciplined under

the higher, the long-drawn-out spiritual disaster had actually begun to take effect upon the germ plasm; so that individuals were doomed before birth to lassitude, and to mentality in a minor key. The First Men, long ago, had fallen into a kind of racial senility through a combination of vulgar errors and indulgences. But the second species, like a boy whose mind has been too soon burdened with grave experience, lived henceforth in a sleep-walk.'

3. When the Second Men had remained in their strange racial trance for about thirty million years, the obscure forces that make for advancement began to stir in them once more. This reawakening was favoured by geological accident. An incursion of the sea gradually isolated some of their number in an island continent, which was once part of the North Atlantic ocean-bed. The climate of this island gradually cooled from sub-tropical to temperate and sub-arctic. The vast change of conditions caused in the imprisoned race a subtle chemical re-arrangement of the germ plasm, such that there ensued an epidemic of biological variation. Many new types appeared, but in the long run one, more vigorous and better adapted than the rest, crowded out all competitors and slowly consolidated itself as a new species, the Third Men.'

In Chapter VII, 3 (p. 145) Stapledon describes the ever-increasing brain growth of the Second Men as similar to the phenomenon of tusk development in the sabre-toothed tiger. How well does the case of the sabre-toothed tiger fit Stapledon's argument? (Answering this question will probably involve a bit of library research; try, among others, G. Simpson's *The Major Features of Evolution* for a discussion of the sabre-toothed tiger.) What would have happened if the new variation to roomier skulls had turned out to be a recessive Mendelian character rather than the dominant one that Stapledon envisages?

Points for discussion or essays

Discuss whether man at the present time should engage in *any* eugenic programs (either of the 'positive' or of the 'negative' strategy).

As one of the First Men, what is your response to the moral, esthetic and scientific dimensions of the 'plastic vital art' (Chapter X, 3) practiced by the Third Men upon the fauna of the planet?

With their increased ability to manipulate the genetic material, the Third Men finally turned their efforts upon man himself. What is most distinctive in man is mind, so they chose to 'breed strictly for brain, for intelligent coordination of behavior'. The results of this attempt were the Great Brains, who first helped, then enslaved, and at last exterminated their creators. The Great Brains, however, ultimately turned their cool intellects upon themselves, and in recognizing their failings, ventured to create a superior species, the Fifth Men. As Stapledon says of these Fifth Men 'they were the first to attain true human proportions of body and mind'. With their accomplishments in art, science and philosophy; their telepathic powers which allowed them to empathize with each other in a way impossible for us First Men; and their ability to travel mentally back through time to experience the whole of previous human existence, the Fifth Men became the most perfect species ever to dwell on earth. Discuss whether, in human terms, the nobility of the Fifth Men is worth the price of the Great Brains.

Stapledon's Neptunian narrator briefly skims over the Third Men's earliest attempts at genetic engineering:

> At first they produced innumerable tragic abortions. These we need not observe. But at length, several thousand years after the earliest experiments, something was produced which seemed to promise success. (Chapter XI, 1)

It is indeed reasonably certain that attempts at improving mankind by manipulation of the genetic material would produce a large number of 'failures', especially in the early stages of research. Success, on the other hand, would mean not just a generalized (and what might seem an abstract) improvement of the species, it would also mean the prevention, or embryonic correction, of debilitating hereditary defects. Discuss under what circumstances (if any) genetic engineering should be pursued. What about the attempts by means of such genetic engineering to prepare man for a new world if the old becomes uninhabitable because of events beyond man's power to prevent (e.g. the Venusians designing men fit for Neptune, or the Last Men's efforts to create and disseminate a human seed in the galaxy)?

Compare and contrast Stapledon's treatment of man's 'vital engineering' with that of Mary Shelley in *Frankenstein*.

Chapter Five
Aldous Huxley: Prospero of a Shakespeareless New World

In *Literature and Science*, an essay on closing the gap between the 'two cultures', Aldous Huxley asserts that the facts and theories of science enable the twentieth century man of letters to treat the theme of human destiny with a depth of understanding of which his predecessors were incapable. A number of Aldous Huxley's own literary efforts, and especially *Brave New World*, give support to his thesis. It is difficult to imagine another author in a more promising position to attempt a literary employment of scientific conceptions; both heredity and environment seemed to groom Huxley for such a task. Grandson of T. H. Huxley (who exerted so strong an influence on H. G. Wells), and brother of the eminent contemporary evolutionary biologist, Julian Huxley, Aldous demonstrated a lifelong concern with both science and literature. Were it not for his poor eyesight, he might well have become a scientist himself. In an early book on travel he remarks:

> If I could be born again and choose what I should be in my next existence, I should desire to be a man of science . . . The only thing that might make me hesitate would be an offer by fate of artistic genius. But even if I could be Shakespeare, I think I should still choose to be Faraday.

As his many successful novels testify, Huxley was, in fact, granted a large share of artistic genius. He retained his early interest in science as well, but his artistic and humanistic concerns broadened this interest to include a trenchant criticism of the misuses of science and technology, which should be applied as though 'they had been made for man, not . . . as though man were to be adapted and enslaved to them'.

In *Brave New World* Huxley combines his concerns about the human uses of science and technology with the philosophical preoccupations that run through most of his novels of twentieth century manners and morals — preoccupations that typically force his characters to take dichotomous positions, as between truth or beauty and happiness, or between puritanical sexual repression and infantile promiscuity. Philip Thody, in his biographical study of Huxley's work, argues that the science fiction form provided him with a particularly effective device for an unconventional treatment of the problems of the human condition:

> What one might call the main philosophical theme in *Brave New*

World is a very personal element in the novel, and its emotional impact stems from the fact that Huxley, perhaps without fully realizing what he was doing, made use of the apparently impersonal genre of a science fiction fantasy to express a deeply felt personal dilemma. 'A world in which ideas did not exist would be a happy world', he wrote. *Brave New World* loses its irony when placed in the context both of Huxley's early work and of his later, mystical development. Since only unhappy people produce literature . . . since human life requires such misery if the specifically human activities of art and science are to continue, might it not be preferable to end the requirement whereby man must live an animal existence on human terms . . . and thus destroy the unhappiness which has so far been the unjustifiably high price which he has had to pay for being human?

This kind of question is not one which literature normally asks. Not only is it too naive, but the problem of inserting it into a convincing account of how people actually behave is quite insuperable . . . the very suggestion that people could be happy if they tried is as ridiculous as the idea that they might all suddenly levitate or start to play cricket. The suggestion could only be seriously developed in a work benefiting from the science fiction convention that all things logically possible are also technically feasible. Huxley's exploitation of science fiction as a medium for the expression of ideas provides, in this respect, perhaps the final step in the acquisition for this genre of its literary *lettres de noblesse*.

Like Stapledon, then, Huxley is using science fiction as a vehicle for philosophical speculation. Huxley's use of the genre was not a one-time only 'sport' of his creative imagination; he clearly used the form in similar fashion in his later *Ape and Essence* and, at least arguably, in *After Many a Summer* and *Island*. And H. G. Wells exerted his influence here as well, albeit negatively: *Brave New World* started out as a parody of Wells' optimistic projection of the future, *Men Like Gods*, though it ended up being a characteristically personal statement.

Many of the best effects of satire are obtained by the tension between unlikely elements and the eminently believable. In this respect, Huxley has gone to great pains to make the scientific and technological foundations of his future society as convincing as possible. Joseph Needham, himself a biochemist as well as a historian of science, said in a review of *Brave New World* that the biologist has 'a sardonic smile as he reads it' because

he knows that the biology is perfectly right . . . Successful experiments are even now being made in the cultivation of embryos

49

of small mammals *in vitro*, and one of the most horrible of Mr Huxley's predictions, the production of low grade workers of precisely identical genetic constitution from one egg, is perfectly possible.

Now, four decades after the book and Needham's review, many of Huxley's biological extrapolations seem not just possible, but imminent. The insights of cell biology and genetics have led to a picture of embryonic development couched in chemical as well as biological terms. The fertilized egg, containing hereditary material from both parents in its chromosomes, is viewed as undergoing a precisely regulated process of reproduction and development; large numbers of cells are produced, all carrying identical genetic information, which differentiate into highly diverse forms with specialized functions as a result of their response to subtle differences in their chemical environments. While the phenomenon of embryonic development is still awe-inspiring, its mystery has been reduced by the apparent success of biochemical explanations for parts of the process. Concomitantly it no longer appears inviolate as an object for scientific study or experimentation. This philosophical revaluation of the nature of human development is a necessary starting point for both Stapledon's and Huxley's treatment of biological engineering.

Work at the University of Cambridge has already taken us several tentative steps toward the 'test-tube' baby. It is now possible to excise ovarian tissue containing egg cells in a relatively minor operation (on women with certain types of infertility who have volunteered in the hopes of being able to bear their own children), to mature these oocytes in a chemical culture medium, to fertilize them with donor sperm, and to grow these fertilized eggs *in vitro* up to the blastocyst stage (that is, beyond the third division of the zygote, or the eight-cell configuration). If this process can be continued through the fifth or sixth zygotic division, producing an embryo of around 100 cells, without abnormal development occurring, it is quite likely that such an embryo could be successfully implanted in the original donor of the egg or, perhaps, in a surrogate mother. While some technical problems remain, the full process has been successfully carried out in at least one mammalian species, the mouse, with apparently normal young rodents, blissfully unaware of their scientific notability, as the result. Because of the economic importance of a serviceable technique of this sort, in for example, the raising of livestock, it may be expected that the research will continue.*

Equivalent success in growing an embryo outside the uterus is rather more distant, although rat and rabbit embryos have been nurtured for several days beyond the time when they would normally implant in the uterus. Merely having a developing embryo available for a certain time before implantation, however, offers a very considerable potential for biological engineering and intervention. Even at the present level of technology (assuming only successful implantation of human embryos in the uterus) researchers in the area can seriously discuss a number of possibilities. Since there could be several fertilized oocytes from one couple, one could exercise selection in deciding which one to return to the mother, so that sex of the baby could be predetermined. In the case of sex-linked genetic diseases like hemophilia, this would prevent the appearance of the abnormal phenotype. More important, though more difficult, is the possibility of introducing into the embryo at a very early stage donor cells which could 'colonize' and assimilate with the native cells; to some extent this has already been achieved in mouse embryos. If the donor cells carried good copies of genes for which the embryo was defective, such colonization of the embryo might allow for the correction of the effects of genetic abnormalities. In many ways this may be the most promising approach to biological engineering in the near future. Thus, deliberate intervention in embryonic development, *a la* Huxley, is an easily contemplatable proposal at the present time.

Bokanovsky's Process, the production of up to 96 identical human beings from one fertilized egg, does not appear close to realization if one considers it in the *exact* form that Huxley projected. But with only slight modification of the specifics of the process, Huxley's picture of a world of duplicated individuals bears a disturbingly prescient resemblance to popular accounts, forty years later, of the possible results of the highly dramatic technique of 'cloning' (which will be discussed more fully in the notes to Chapter 6).

Both Stapledon and Huxley consider questions of human destiny by exploring the potentialities and consequences of remaking man in one or another image. There are superficial points of difference in the details of their extrapolations, of course; Stapledon, for example, assumes that man is remade primarily through manipulation of the hereditary material, while Huxley projects controlled fertilization followed by manipulation of the growing embryo. But the fundamental

---

*The pace and climate of work in this area may be gauged from recent events. As this book was being completed, D. Bevis, Professor of Obstetrics and Gynaecology at Leeds University, announced at the scientific meeting of the British Medical Association (15 July 1974) that several babies had been born successfully following test-tube fertilization and implantation in the mothers. On 19 July 1974, *The Guardian* reported further ramifications of the work: It pointed out that 'it is a technique that depends greatly on chance, and he also had many failures'. It also disclosed that Professor Bevis was giving up research in this field because of the pressure of publicity which included an 'offer from a national newspaper to pay him a large sum' (rejected, but variously reported as £30 000–£50 000) 'to disclose the identity of the test-tube babies . . . Research workers in this field have agreed that if secrecy is not observed, 'test-tube babies' would be exposed to curiosity and even ridicule for the rest of their lives.'

difference of their approaches — and the catholicity of viewpoint permitted by the science fiction form — may best be illustrated by a short Stapledonian episode in the history of the Third Men:

> The world community was now a highly organized theocratic hierarchy, strictly but on the whole benevolently ruled by a supreme council of vital priests and biologists. Each individual, down to the humblest agricultural worker, had his special niche in society, allotted him by the supreme council or its delegates, according to his known heredity and the needs of society. This system, of course, sometimes led to abuse, but mostly it worked without serious friction. Such was the precision of biological knowledge that each person's mental calibre and special aptitudes were known beyond dispute, and rebellion against his lot in society would have been rebellion against his own heredity. This fact was universally known, and accepted without regret. (Chapter X, 4)

What for one author, then, may be a throw-away idea treated in the space of a single paragraph, can by another be developed into the controlling theme for an entire novel.

Sources

Birnbaum, M. (1971). *Aldous Huxley's Quest for Values*. Knoxville, Tennessee, U. of Tennessee Press

Edwards, R. G. and Fowler, R. E. (1970). 'Human Embryos in the Laboratory'. *Scientific American*, Dec.

Firchow, P. (1972). *Aldous Huxley*. Minneapolis, U. of Minnesota Press

May, K. (1972). *Aldous Huxley*. London, Elek

Thody, P. (1973). *Aldous Huxley*. London, Studio Vista

Unsigned review (1969). 'Embryos outside the Body'. *Nature, Lond.* **223**, 6 Sept

Reading

ESSENTIAL

Huxley, A. *Brave New World*. London, Penguin; New York, Perennial Library, Harper and Row

RELATED

Aldiss, B. (1973). *Billion Year Spree*. London, Weidenfeld; Garden City, N.Y., Doubleday
See Chapter 8 'In the Name of the Zeitgeist: Mainly the Thirties.'

Birnbaum, M. (1971). *Aldous Huxley's Quest for Values.* Knoxville, Tennessee, U. of Tennessee Press
See Chapter IX 'Science and Technology'.

Edwards, R. G. and Fowler, R. E. (1970). 'Human Embryos in the Laboratory.' *Scientific American,* Dec.
'It is now possible to make human eggs mature, to fertilize them *in vitro* and to grow them in a culture medium through early embryonic stages. Such procedures may help to alleviate infertility and fetal abnormalities.'

Edwards, R. G. and Sharpe, D. J. (1971). 'Social Values and Research in Human Embryology.' *Nature, Lond.* **231,** 14 May
'New techniques for interfering with the early stages of human development raise difficult social and legal issues which are discussed here by an embryologist (in fact, the major investigator in this line of research) and a lawyer.'

Friedmann, T. (1971). 'Prenatal Diagnosis of Genetic Disease.' *Scientific American,* Nov.
'New techniques are making it possible to detect hereditary diseases early in pregnancy. To what extent is the control of such births justified on biological and social grounds?'

Grossman, E. (1971). 'The Obsolescent Mother.' *Atlantic,* May
A non-technical account of the recent work on *in vitro* fertilization and embryonic growth with an interesting discussion of its social and political implications.

Huxley, A. *After Many a Summer.* London, Penguin; New York, Perennial Library, Harper and Row
Huxley's witty variant of the search-for-immortality theme.

Huxley, A. *Island.* London, Penguin; New York, Perennial Library, Harper and Row
Huxley's valedictory Utopia.

Huxley, A. (1963). *Literature and Science.* London, Chatto; New York, Harper and Row
Huxley's contribution to the Leavis—Snow debate on the 'two cultures'.

May, K. (1972). *Aldous Huxley.* London, Elek
See Chapter 5 *Brave New World.*

Orwell, G. *1984.* London, Penguin; New York, Signet, NAL
Ranks with *Brave New World* as the most famous future dystopia.

Thody, P. (1973). *Aldous Huxley.* London, Studio Vista
See Chapter 4 *Brave New World.*

Wells, H. G. (1923). *Men Like Gods.* London, Cassell
To quote Aldiss: 'A Mr. Barnstaple drives in his car into the fourth dimension and there finds a Utopia of beautiful and powerful (and frequently nude) people.'

Wells, H. G. (1909). *A Modern Utopia*. London, Nelson; Lincoln, Nebraska, Nebraska UP (1967)

'No less than a planet will serve the purpose of a modern Utopia,' writes Wells. In this curious blend of novel and tract, he conjures up an alternate Earth identical to ours in all respects save its socio-political system.

Zamyatin, E. *We*. London, Penguin; New York, Bantam

An earlier (1920) version of a future to despair; closer in attitude and tone to Orwell than to Huxley.

Unsigned editorial (1971). 'Rules and Regulations for Test-tube Babies.' *Nature, Lond.* **231**, 14 May

The editorial apparently reflects a professional's response to the legal and philosophical problems of human embryological research — set up an advisory body of 'internationally known professionals'.

Unsigned review (1971). 'Embryos outside the Body.' *Nature, Lond.* **231**, 14 May

Very good summary of the work in the area; slightly technical but quite readable.

Questions

How essential is the scientific background to the effective expression of the points that Huxley wishes to make in *Brave New World*?

In his preface, written some fifteen years after the original publication of *Brave New World*, Huxley criticizes himself for having provided only two alternatives, 'an insane life in Utopia, or the life of a primitive in an Indian village.' If the book were to be rewritten, he would offer the savage a third alternative, a possibility of sanity. Would this strengthen or weaken the effect of the book? Why?

Is *Brave New World* compatible with a Marxist critique of society? The world of 632 After Ford is obviously a class society, but is it a Capitalist class society? Since the system does, in a sense, exemplify the principle 'from each according to his ability; to each according to his needs', can it be argued that it is, in fact, a Marxist society?

Points for discussion or essays

Compare and contrast Huxley's and Stapledon's treatment of the theme of human biological engineering.

Compare and contrast the literary devices which Huxley uses to present the necessary background information for his future society with the techniques employed by Stapledon and Wells for theirs.

Both Wells and Huxley enjoyed a considerable literary reputation outside the science fiction field on the basis of their mainstream novels of modern life. Judging their science fiction works by traditional literary criteria, who is the superior writer?

Huxley began *Brave New World* as a parody of Wells' Utopian *Men Like Gods*. Wells later said: '*Brave New World* was a great disappointment to me. A writer of the standing of Aldous Huxley has no right to betray the future as he did in that book. When thinking about the future, people seem to overlook the logical progress in education, in architecture, and science.' Discuss the validity of Wells' criticism.

If one must choose in the Savage/World Controller debate (Chapters 16 and 17), which position is the better answer for human needs?

Compose a debate over the value of the post-Fordian society between Mustapha Mond and Olaf Stapledon.

Compare Huxley's treatment of the future of man in *Brave New World* with that in his later *Ape and Essence*.

Is Huxley's *Brave New World* really such a dystopia? Compare and contrast Huxley's version of future society with another (dystopic) twentieth century work, such as Eugene Zamyatin's *We* or George Orwell's *1984*.

Wells and Huxley entered the science fiction field as anti-Utopian writers; yet both men later turned to more positive Utopian projections (Wells in such works as *A Modern Utopia* and *Men Like Gods*, the latter provoking Huxley's *Brave New World*, which was itself followed thirty years later by his Utopic *Island*.) Discuss this seemingly parallel evolution in the thought of the two authors with reference to one Utopian and one anti-Utopian work of each.

Chapter Six
Blish, Le Guin, Wilhelm and Wolfe: Four Heads for a Science Fiction Watchdog

Both Stapledon and Huxley based their extrapolations of man's future upon the belief that increasing biological knowledge would ultimately lead to the possibility of consciously remaking man by genetic or embryonic manipulation. The developments in biology in the last two decades have not robbed these literary projections of their impact, but rather made them even more immediate. Phrases like 'Skills for Genetic Engineers', 'Gene Insertion into Mammalian Cells' and 'Gene Therapy for Human Genetic Disease' are no longer the trappings for a science fiction novel — they are the titles of articles that have appeared in scientific journals in the past few years. What has transformed a science fiction theme into the subject for professional scientific concern is the rise and phenomenal success of a new approach to biology — a 'molecular biology' in which the basic processes of the living cell are studied at the molecular level. This approach has provided an increasingly detailed understanding of the material basis of heredity and development; progress in this area has been so rapid as to exceed the wildest speculations of most biologists carrying on research at the time Stapledon's and Huxley's novels were written.

The event which crystallized this revolution in biology was the elucidation in 1953 by James Watson and Francis Crick of the structure of the DNA molecule; this discovery is probably the most important occurrence in biology since the introduction of Darwin's theory itself. It had previously been known that the chromosomes, the presumed carriers of genetic information in the cell, were composed almost equally of protein and DNA. For a number of technical reasons it had long been believed that the actual genetic material must be the protein portion of the chromosomes, but evidence favoring the opposite interpretation had been slowly building up, and Watson and Crick's 'double helix' model of DNA laid the controversy finally to rest. The DNA molecule is an immensely long chain of subunits called 'nucleotides'; the DNA in a chromosome may consist of ten million or more of these nucleotides linked together in linear fashion. There are, however, only four different kinds of nucleotide subunit. The DNA molecule may be considered a chemical 'message' written with these four characters; it is their order or sequence along the molecule which makes one man different from another, and both from a fruit fly. (By analogy, the most complicated human messages can be expressed with the use of 26 characters by a literate writer of English, or with only two characters by a trained telegrapher.) The importance of their discovery cannot be overemphasized: all man's hereditary physical characteristics — and probably, most of his mental abilities as well — are the result of the arrangement of four specific nucleotides in individual chemical molecules of DNA. The replacement of *one* nucleotide by another in a chain millions of nucleotides long is often the difference between a normal life and one terminated by a fatal genetic abnormality.

A coherent picture of the genetic control of the life processes emerged. The master blueprint for the functioning of every cell resides in the DNA of that cell. RNA molecules, which are working copies of the DNA blueprint, are transcribed from the DNA in the nucleus and migrate to the cytoplasm where the protein-synthesizing apparatus of the cell is located. Here the RNA message is translated in a virtually automatic fashion into a specific protein, generally an enzyme; a sequence of three nucleotides in the RNA causes the incorporation of a particular amino acid (the basic building block of proteins) into a lengthening protein chain. Most of the thousands of essential bio-chemical reactions that go on every second in a living organism will not take place without the presence of specific catalysts, one for each of the different reactions; thus the control of the life processes is via the specific activity of the catalytic enzyme proteins whose detailed structure is directly determined by the genetic information contained in the DNA of the chromosomes. The 'gene', that previously mysterious and highly abstract conception, was now realized to be a short section, a few thousand nucleotide units long, of a DNA molecule.

Since all the cells of a human being are descended from a single fertilized egg, they presumably contain the same genetic information in their chromosomes. But nerve cells are obviously different in appearance and function from muscle cells, and both of these from skin cells, etc. It must be the case, then, that a single cell uses only a small percentage of the total genetic information it contains, transcribing into RNA and translating into protein only those portions of the DNA relevant to its specific cellular functions; the greatest part of the DNA in those cells must be 'turned off'. The enormously complex process of development from a fertilized egg can be viewed as a finely orchestrated sequence of turning on and turning off different portions of the DNA in embryonic cells as they differentiate into the specialized cell types. Although many of the details of the genetic control of function and development are yet to be revealed, most molecular biologists feel they have reached an understanding of the fundamental principles involved.

It is this understanding, at the molecular level, that provides for the first time a basis for realistic and detailed speculation about the possibilities of genetic engineering. It seems extremely unlikely, for example, that controlled alteration of a zygotic or germ-cell gene — by manipulation of a single nucleotide or of a small number of nucleotides —

could be achieved in the forseeable future. Another approach, however, might be the introduction of a new piece of DNA to replace an undesired or defective gene. For a number of years it had been possible to accomplish this to some limited extent in bacteria; but more recently it has been discovered that a particularly easy method of introducing new genetic information, termed 'plasmid engineering', exists for cells of *E. coli,* the common intestinal bacterium which has been the molecular biologist's favorite research organism.*

A related technique, perhaps more directly applicable to human rather than bacterial cells, is the possibility of introducing natural or artificial genetic information by attaching this to the DNA or RNA of a presumably harmless 'carrier' virus which would spread through the target cells. In fact, a therapeutic use of this technique has already been attempted with human patients — two children suffering from argininemia, a hereditary deficiency of the enzyme arginase (which normally breaks down excess concentrations of arginine); the high level of arginine in the blood and cerebrospinal fluid generally results in severe mental retardation, associated epilepsy and other metabolic abnormalities. There was some early evidence which suggested that the Shope papilloma virus (which induces warts on the skin of rabbits, but has no symptomatic effects in man) carried the genetic information for an arginase enzyme. It was hoped that introducing such genetic information by means of the virus carrier might cause the patients to manufacture higher levels of arginase and so ameliorate their disability; no change in their condition was reported, however. An alternative approach to biological engineering might follow upon a more detailed understanding of the mechanisms for turning on and turning off sections of DNA. Combined with an ability to grow an

---

*In the same week that produced the report of the first successful test-tube babies, a group of 11 American chemists and biochemists, supported in an unprecedented step by the most prestigious body of scientists in the US — the National Academy of Science — made an announcement which seemed to be modelled directly upon a now-disdained plot device from the days of the science fiction 'pulps'. *The Guardian* (19 July 1974) reported that the scientists urged 'a worldwide halt to a type of genetic research because they fear that the work could lead to the creation and the possible escape of an unknown, dangerously infectious strain of bacteria that could cause uncontrollable epidemics.' The National Academy statement itself points out in only slightly more cautious terms: Several groups of scientists are now planning to use this technology . . . Although such experiments are likely to facilitate the solution of important theoretical and practical biological problems, they would also result in the creation of novel types of infectious DNA elements whose biological properties cannot be completely predicted in advance. There is serious concern that some of these artificial recombinant DNA molecules could prove biologically hazardous.' Because *E. coli* is the most common member of the human intestinal flora, and exists to some degree in interchange with the environment, the concern is that a harmful strain of the bacterium 'might possibly become widely disseminated among human, bacterial, plant or animal populations with unpredictable effects.'

embryo for some period of time *in vitro,* this knowledge could make it possible to manipulate embryonic development, in a Huxleyan fashion, by skilful alteration of the chemical environments of the differentiating cells.

One of the more sensational developments in recent biological research has been the well-publicized phenomenon of 'cloning', first carried out some ten years ago at the University of Oxford. An unfertilized egg is subjected to ultraviolet irradiation so as to destroy its own nucleus. A donor nucleus is taken from a tadpole intestinal cell and transplanted into the enucleated egg cell; since the intestinal cell nucleus contains the double set of chromosomes characteristic of all body cells, the egg cell now has the same number of chromosomes as a normally fertilized zygote. Although most of the embryos formed by this technique develop abnormally, about 1.5% of the eggs with transplanted nuclei produce fully normal adult frogs of the strain represented by the donor of the transplanted nucleus. What this demonstrates is that differentiated cells (like the tadpole intestinal cell) contain all the genetic information present in the original zygote from which they were produced; and in some cases, at least, they can de-differentiate so as to have turned on portions of their DNA that were previously turned off. The nuclear transplantation process can, in addition, be carried on serially. The egg that has received a donor nucleus can be allowed to develop only to the blastula stage; the genetically identical nuclei from these cells can then be further transplanted into enucleate recipient eggs to form a clone, a population of genetically identical individuals. The process could theoretically be continued at will, resulting in any desired number of 'carbon-copy' individuals. In principle, then, the limit of 96 genetically identical individuals producible by Bokanovsky's Process in *Brave New World* seems far too conservative.

It should be emphasized that at the present time this operation has been successfully carried out only on certain amphibian species, whose eggs are large and relatively easy to work with and do not require a uterus in which to develop. Nevertheless, progress in certain cell fusion techniques, and particularly the work on fertilization and embryonic growth of mammalian eggs *in vitro* (discussed in the material of Chapter 5) have made the idea of cloned humans a possibility to be taken seriously. James Watson predicts that 'if the matter proceeds in its current non-directed fashion, a human being born of clonal reproduction most likely will appear on the earth within the next twenty to fifty years, and even sooner, if some nation should actively promote the venture.'

The present successes and probable future developments of molecular biology and embryology form the scientific backdrop to the work of the four authors being considered here. The stories of James Blish, 'Seeding Program' and 'Watershed', first published in 1955, furnish an interesting transition between the Stapledonian treatment of the theme of genetic engineering and the manner in which it has been handled by Le Guin, Wolfe and Wilhelm much more recently. Blish's stories have been quite consciously based on a Stapledonian conception. 'Seeding Program' (and the collection from which it is taken, *The Seedling Stars*) clearly derives from the final project of the Last Men on Neptune: 'In respect of the future we are now setting about the forlorn task of disseminating among the stars the seeds of a new humanity.' Blish invokes Stapledon himself (albeit somewhat backhandedly) by pointing out that 'the notion of modifying the human stock genetically to live on the planets as they were found, rather than changing the planets to accommodate the people, had been old with Olaf Stapledon . . .' Similarly, Hoqqueah in 'Watershed' expresses the Stapledonian view that C. S. Lewis so strongly deplored:

> There's no survival value in pinning one's race forever to one set of specs. It's only sensible to go on evolving with the universe, so as to stay independent of such things as the aging of worlds, or the explosions of their suns. And look at the results. Man exists now in so many forms that there's always a refuge *somewhere* for any threatened people.

Blish differs from Stapledon, however, in that his examination of the problems of remaking man is carried on at the level of individual human responses. We see the emotional concomitants of being an 'adapted man' in an Earth-normal society; and we explore the reactions of unmodified men to the adapted 'others'. And in 'Watershed', the brief coda to *The Seedling Stars*, Blish confronts directly the philosophical question raised by all suggestions of remaking man: What is the essential nature of humanity?

It is these kinds of concerns that characterize much of the best science fiction writing of recent years and which figure so fundamentally in the stories by Ursula Le Guin, Gene Wolfe and Kate Wilhelm. Both 'Nine Lives' and 'The Fifth Head of Cerberus' deal with the philosophical and emotional problems of cloning: What is the psychological state of a human being who has been cloned? How does a non-duplicated individual react to one who has been cloned? And, perhaps most subtle question of all, what does cloning do, not just to the cloned, but to the cloners? It is this latter concern that is the central preoccupation of 'The Planners'; here the type of genetic engineering is different — RNA transfer rather than cloning — but the human questions are the same. All three of these stories can be read as an examination of the borderline between human and nonhuman, a once clear-cut distinction that the progress of modern biology has made far more problematic.

These stories reflect a recent development in science fiction, often termed the 'new wave' — the use of outer space as a device for exploring inner space. The technical details are important not for their own sake so much as to provide new perspectives or new settings for an exploration of human problems and human choices. The emphasis is on craftsmanship in literary construction and on the portrayal of psychologically realistic (though at the same time imaginatively projected) beings, whether human, adapted or alien. That these values are shared by a majority of the practicing science fiction writers at the present time is shown by the fact that these stories by Le Guin, Wolfe and Wilhelm are all Nebula Award winners or runners-up, a highly regarded professional accolade voted annually by the three hundred members of the Science Fiction Writers Association.

Sources

Friedman, T. and Roblin, R. (1972). 'Gene Therapy for Human Genetic Disease?' *Science*, **175**, 3 March

Gurdon, J. B. (1968). 'Transplanted Nuclei and Cell Differentiation.' *Scientific American*, Dec.

Rogers, S. (1970). 'Skills for Genetic Engineers.' *New Scientist*, 29 Jan.

Watson, J. D. (1971). 'Moving Toward the Clonal Man.' *Atlantic*, May

Readings

ESSENTIAL

Blish, J. (1967). *The Seedling Stars.* London, Faber; New York, NAL (1972)
Book 1: 'Seeding Program' and Book 4: 'Watershed'.

Le Guin, U. (1969). 'Nine Lives'. In *Playboy*; also in *Nebula Award Stories Five* and *The Wind's Twelve Quarters,* 1975 variously available among UK and US hardback and paperback editions

Wilhelm, K. 'The Planners'. In *Orbit 3, The Downstairs Room,* and *The Best from Orbit* variously available among UK and US hardback and paperback editions

Wolfe, G. (1976). 'The Fifth Head of Cerberus'. New York, Ace. Also in *Orbit 10,* variously available among UK and US hardback and paperback editions

RELATED

Borek, E. (1965). *The Code of Life.* New York, Columbia UP
A good popularization of the basics of molecular biology; particularly useful for readers without a background in biology.

Friedmann, T. and Roblin, R. (1972). 'Gene Therapy for Human Genetic Disease?' *Science,* **175,** 3 March
The difficult scientific and ethical problems raised by proposals for genetic manipulation in humans.

Fletcher, J. (1971). 'Ethical Aspects of Genetic Controls.' *New England Journal of Medicine,* **285,** 30 Sept.
A definition of the ethical issue as between those who determine what is right and wrong on *a priori* grounds, often metarational or religious, and those who decide on the basis of consequences; the author defends the latter position.

Gurdon, J. B. (1968). 'Transplanted Nuclei and Cell Differentiation.' *Scientific American,* Dec.
'The nucleus of a cell from a frog's intestine is transplanted into a frog's egg and gives rise to a normal frog. Such experiments aid the study of how genes are controlled during embryonic development.'

Kass, L. R. (1971). 'The New Biology: What Price Relieving Man's Estate?' *Science,* **174,** 19 Nov.
This article should be read as a companion piece to Fletcher's; it is much more critical of the ethical consequences of biological manipulation.

Monod, J. (1972). *Chance and Necessity.* London, Collins; New York, Vintage
The philosophical implications of molecular biology by a leading figure (and Nobel Prizewinner) in the field. A controversial book, attacked by both Catholic and Marxist philosophers.

Moore, J. A. (1972). *Heredity and Development.* London, Oxford UP
Cited in *Related Reading* for Part 2, Chapter 4.

Rogers, S. (1970). 'Skills for Genetic Engineers.' *New Scientist,* 29 Jan.
An excellent short discussion of the techniques now available for fabricating desired genes in the laboratory and introducing them into cells; some use of technical language however.

Stent, G. (1969). *The Coming of the Golden Age: An End to Progress.* Garden City, New York, Natural History Press
Cited in *Related Reading* for Part 1, Chapter 2. The first half of the book is an elegant short summary of the essentials of molecular genetics.

Stern, C. (1973). *Principles of Human Genetics.* San Francisco, Freeman
The most widely-used American textbook on human genetics.

Watson, J. D. (1970). *The Molecular Biology of the Gene.* 2nd edition. New York, Benjamin
A detailed introduction to molecular genetics by the man who unraveled the structure of DNA. Directed at undergraduate biology students; and at this level, probably the best book on the subject.

Watson, J. D. (1971). 'Moving Toward the Clonal Man.' *Atlantic,* May
Predictions and cautions on the possibilities of cloning in a popularly written account.

Questions

How essential is the scientific background to the effective expression of the points of Blish, Le Guin, Wilhelm and Wolfe wish to make?

Does the treatment of experimental nucleic acid (RNA) transfer in 'The Planners' present any opportunities or difficulties that are not present in the stories dealing with cloning ('Nine Lives' and 'Cerberus')?

How has the now-famous 'double helix' structure of DNA been used symbolically in 'The Fifth Head of Cerberus'?

Two further questions may be of interest but will most likely require some library research for students who are not in a biology program:

In 'Nine Lives' one of the characters points out:
> It's easy to program half the clonal mass back to the female. Just delete the male gene (chromosome?) from half the cells and they revert to the basic, that is, the female. It's trickier to go the other way, have to hook in artificial Y chromosomes. So they mostly clone from males, since clones function best bisexually . . . We females are sterile . . . you remember that the Y chromosome was deleted from our original cell.

How consistent is this account with current knowledge in genetics? What are the characteristics of individuals with an extra Y chromosome (XXY or XYY males) or of individuals with only a single X chromosome (XO females)?

Molecular biologists distinguish between messenger RNA (mRNA), transfer or soluble RNA (tRNA or sRNA), and ribosomal RNA (rRNA). What are the different roles of these three types of RNA in the genetic control of cellular activity? Is Wilhelm technically correct in choosing sRNA as the nucleic acid to be used in information transfer experiments?

Points for discussion or essays

Compare and contrast Huxley's and Stapledon's treatment of the theme of human biological engineering in the early 1930s with that of Le Guin, Wilhelm and Wolfe in the late 1960s and early 1970s. Discuss the extent to which their differing treatments are a reflection of changed intellectual, social and technological climates.

In 'Watershed' Hoqqueah notes that 'it was also a very old idea on the Earth that basic humanity inheres in the mind, not in the form'. Discuss this idea with respect to the four authors being considered.

Compare and contrast the positions taken by Blish, Le Guin, Wolfe and Wilhelm as to the benefits and costs of genetic engineering in social and individual human terms.

'Nine Lives' and 'The Fifth Head of Cerberus' both employ cloning as their central device. Compare and contrast the way that Le Guin and Wolfe use this process to explore questions of morality, sociology and psychology.

Discuss 'The Fifth Head of Cerberus' as an examination of the essential qualities that define humanness and/or as a projection of man's fears of depersonalization in a technological age. Include in your discussion the characters of the father, the son (narrator), the aunt, Mr Million, and Marsch, the visiting anthropologist.

'Nine Lives' and 'The Planners' were written by women, *The Seedling Stars* and 'The Fifth Head of Cerberus' by men. Is there a significant difference of technique or attitude between the sexes when writing about biological engineering? (It is interesting in this regard to note that when 'Nine Lives' first appeared in *Playboy*, the editors attributed it to 'U' rather than to 'Ursula' Le Guin.)

Which of the stories is the most effective exploration of the human dimensions of biological engineering? Discuss.

Using the stories of Blish, Le Guin, Wilhelm and Wolfe as a starting point, but extending the discussion with the addition of your own views on the subject, are the possibilities for cloning and nucleic acid transfer cause for optimism or pessimism?